WHAT IN THE WORLD IS GOING ON?

10 Prophetic Clues You Cannot Afford to Ignore

DR. DAVID JEREMIAH

with Dr. David Jeremiah

Edited by William Kruidenier

Unless otherwise indicated, Scripture verses quoted are taken from the NEW KING JAMES VERSION.

Printed in the United States of America.

CONTENTS

ABOUT
DR. DAVID JEREMIAH
AND TURNING POINT

D r. David Jeremiah is the founder of Turning Point, a ministry committed to providing Christians with sound Bible teaching relevant to today's changing times through radio and television broadcasts, audio series, and books. Dr. Jeremiah's commonsense teaching on topics such as family, prayer, worship, angels, and biblical prophecy forms the foundation of Turning Point.

David and his wife, Donna, reside in El Cajon, California, where he is the senior pastor of Shadow Mountain Community Church. David and Donna have four children and ten grandchildren.

In 1982, Dr. Jeremiah brought the same solid teaching to San Diego television that he shares weekly with his congregation. Shortly thereafter, Turning Point expanded its ministry to radio. Dr. Jeremiah's inspiring messages can now be heard worldwide on radio and television.

Because Dr. Jeremiah desires to know his listening audience, he travels nationwide holding "A Night of Encouragement" ministry rallies and Spiritual Enrichment conferences that touch the hearts and lives of many people. According to Dr. Jeremiah, "At some point in time, everyone reaches a turning point; and for every person, that moment is unique, an experience to hold onto forever. There's so much changing in today's world that sometimes it's difficult to choose the right path. Turning Point offers people an understanding of God's Word as well as the opportunity to make a difference in their lives."

Dr. Jeremiah has authored numerous books, including *Escape the Coming Night* (Revelation), *The Handwriting on the Wall* (Daniel), *Overcoming Loneliness, Angels: The Strange and Mysterious Truth, The Joy of Encouragement, Prayer—The Great Adventure, God in You* (Holy Spirit), *Gifts from God* (Parenting), *Jesus' Final Warning, When Your World Falls Apart, Slaying the Giants in Your Life, My Heart's Desire, Sanctuary, Life Wide Open, Searching for Heaven on Earth, The Secret of the Light, Captured by Grace, Discover Paradise, Grace Givers, Why the Nativity?, Signs of Life,* and *What in the World Is Going On?*

About This Study Guide

The purpose of this Turning Point study guide is to reinforce Dr. David Jeremiah's dynamic, in-depth teaching and to aid the reader in applying biblical truth to his or her daily life. This study guide is designed to be used in conjunction with Dr. Jeremiah's *What in the World Is Going On?* audio series, but it may also be used by itself for personal or group study.

Structure of the Lessons

Each lesson is based on one of the messages in the *What in the World Is Going On?* compact disc series and focuses on specific passages in the Bible. Each lesson is composed of the following elements:

- *Outline*

The outline at the beginning of the lesson gives a clear, concise picture of the topic being studied and provides a helpful framework for readers as they listen to Dr. Jeremiah's teaching.

- *Overview*

The overview summarizes Dr. Jeremiah's teaching on the passage being studied in the lesson. Readers should refer to the Scripture passages in their own Bibles as they study the overview.

- *Application*

This section contains a variety of questions designed to help readers dig deeper into the lesson and the Scriptures, and to apply the lesson to their daily lives. For Bible study groups or Sunday school classes, these questions will provide a springboard for group discussion and interaction.

- *Did You Know?*

This section presents a fascinating fact, historical note, or insight that adds a point of interest to the preceding lesson.

Using This Guide for Group Study

The lessons in this study guide are suitable for Sunday school classes, small-group studies, elective Bible studies, or home Bible study groups. Each person in the group should have his or her own study guide.

When possible, the study guide should be used with the corresponding compact disc series. You may wish to assign the study guide as homework prior to the meeting of the group and then use the meeting time to listen to the CD and discuss the lesson.

For Continuing Study

A complete catalog of Dr. Jeremiah's materials for personal and group study is available through Turning Point. To obtain a catalog, additional study guides, or more information about Turning Point, call 1-800-947-1993, go online to www.DavidJeremiah.org, or write to: Turning Point, P.O. Box 3838, San Diego, CA 92163.

Dr. Jeremiah's *Turning Point* program is currently heard or viewed around the world on radio, television, and the Internet in English. *Momento Decisivo*, the Spanish translation of Dr. Jeremiah's messages, can be heard on radio in every Spanish speaking country in the world. In some areas, the television broadcast provides Arabic subtitles.

Contact Turning Point for radio and television program times and stations in your area. Or visit our website at www.DavidJeremiah.org.

WHAT IN THE WORLD IS GOING ON?

A day is coming in the future when shock will arrive with the dawn. The shock will have occurred in daylight hours, of course, in some parts of the world. But in other parts the event causing the shock will occur while millions sleep soundly. They are the ones who will awaken to find their community, their nation, and their world in chaos.

What will precipitate such shock and awe? Not the beginning of a military conflict nor news of a natural disaster claiming thousands of innocent lives. Rather, the news will be of the instantaneous disappearance of hundreds of millions of people off the face of planet earth—something that has never before happened in history. Indeed, the Rapture of the church of Jesus Christ is a one-time event.

What is the Rapture of the Church? It is an event described by the apostle Paul in 1 Thessalonians 4:16–17, when Jesus Christ appears in the sky and calls all true believers, living and deceased, to meet Him in the air. They return to heavenly realms together in order for the Church to avoid a seven-year period of tribulation and trouble (referred to in the Old Testament as Jacob's, or Israel's, trouble—Jeremiah 30:7) that is coming upon earth.

A charismatic and Satan-inspired leader will assume leadership of world governments and use the opportunity to attempt to rid the world of the Jewish nation once and for all. In order to save Israel from annihilation, Christ and His army of saints and angels returns to the earth at the end of the Tribulation period to defeat the evil leader, the Antichrist. Christ then establishes His own throne to rule over the nations of the earth for a thousand years—the period of peace and righteousness foreseen by the prophets of old. At the end of that millennial period, Satan is judged and cast into hell where he joins the Antichrist who was consigned there 1,000 years earlier—where they and all the ungodly of history will live in punishment forever.

If the scenes in that scenario are unfamiliar to you—or perhaps familiar but not clear—then this study guide is for you. *What in the World Is Going On?* presents a panoramic sweep of the future according to biblical prophecy. The chapters follow a chronological progression of events that includes every major point remaining to be fulfilled on the biblical timeline.

The study guide begins where all biblical prophecy is rooted: the promises of God to Abraham and his descendants. It is God's plan for Israel that controls the future. They are His chosen people, and many promises made to them remain to be fulfilled. Everything experienced by the Gentile nations of the world in the future will be tied in some way to God's plans for Israel.

After studying ancient foundations in the promises to Abraham, the study jumps to the present with an analysis of the "crude awakening" the world is experiencing with the price of oil—and the implications of the fact that the majority of the world's oil is controlled by nations unfriendly to Israel.

From there it's on to the future: the revival of the ancient Roman Empire, the rise of radical Islam, the Rapture itself, the role of America in prophecy, the Antichrist, a future axis of evil that will attack Israel, the world's final great battle, and the arrival of the King of Kings and Lord of Lords.

If you want to understand a lot of what is going on in the world now and all of what will go on in the future, *What in the World Is Going On?* will provide the biblical answers you seek.

THE ISRAEL CONNECTION

Genesis 12:1–3

*In this lesson we learn how and why Israel
was regathered to her Promised Land.*

OUTLINE

The land of Palestine has been the most embattled in the history of
the world. After 1,900 years of living as refugees around the world,
in 1948 Israel was restored to her homeland. Not all are happy
with her presence there, but Israel is finally back in the land God
promised would be hers.

I. The Record of Israel's Land
 A. God's Choice of Israel
 B. God's Covenant with Israel

II. The Relocation of the People of Israel
 A. The Scattering of the Jewish People
 B. The Suffering of the Jewish People

III. The Rebirth of the Nation of Israel

IV. The Return to the God of Israel

J ust a few minutes before 4:00 p.m. on May 14, 1948, David Ben-Gurion drove down Rothschild Boulevard in Tel Aviv, Israel. Ben-Gurion stepped into the modern two-story building which housed an art museum. There he found some 400 individuals gathered, comprised of Jewish religious and political leaders as well as press representatives from all over the world. Precisely at 4:00 p.m. local time, Ben-Gurion called the meeting to order and read these historic words:

> It is self-evident the right of Jewish people to be a nation as all other nations, its own sovereign state. Accordingly, we meet in solemn assembly today, thus, by virtue of the natural and historic right of the Jewish people and the resolution of the General Assembly of the United Nations. We hereby proclaim the establishment of the Jewish State in Palestine to be called the State of Israel.[1]

The words of Ben-Gurion remind us of the words of the prophet Isaiah who, 740 years before the birth of Jesus, said, "Who has heard such a thing? Who has seen such things? Shall the earth be made to give birth in one day? Or shall a nation be born at once?" (Isaiah 66:8).

On May 14th, 1948, God made good on His promise to Israel by restoring her to the Promised Land. Incredible as it sounds, the existence of Israel today is the number one evidence for the fact that Bible prophecy will be fulfilled literally. According to biblical prophecy, Israel's rebirth as a nation sets in motion the rest of all of the end-time prophecies. Israel's national revival was a necessary prerequisite to the final act of human history.

To understand what happened on that day in May, 1948, and what is happening today in Israel, and what will happen to her in the future, we have to go all the way back to the book of Genesis. Eleven chapters deal with creation, the fall of man, and human history until Abraham, and then the rest of the book (forty-one chapters) deals with Abraham and his descendants. In Genesis 12:1–3 we find God promising Abraham three things: He would be blessed, his name would be great, and he would be a blessing to "all the families of the earth." Those blessings include the written Word of God (written mostly by Jews) and the living Word of God, Jesus, the Messiah.

In His promise to Abraham, God said He would "bless those who bless you, and . . . curse him who curses you" (verse 3). Whether in ancient or modern times, it has never been a good idea to oppose or attack Israel. Part of America's blessing from God is no doubt due to our standing by Israel since her reestablishment as a nation in 1948.

The Record of Israel's Land

Control of the land called Palestine (ancient Canaan; the Promised Land) is the most volatile issue in international geo-political debate. But the land belongs to God, and He deeded it to Israel as her homeland (Genesis 12:7). And that deed has never been cancelled.

God's Choice of Israel

William Ewer was a British journalist to whom is attributed this famous couplet: "How odd of God, to choose the Jews." His words raise the important question of why God chose the Jews, or specifically, Abraham, to be a blessing to all the people on earth.

First, Deuteronomy 7:7 says God did not choose the Jews because they were more numerous than other nations. Even today, Jews comprise less than one percent of the world's population. Second, Isaiah 45:4 supports the idea that God did not choose the Jews because of their spiritual sensitivity to God. And third, Deuteronomy 9:6–7 makes it clear that the Jews weren't chosen because of their righteousness.

In summary, we can see that God didn't choose the Jews because of any of the reasons we might have chosen a people. Rather, God chose Abraham and his descendants on the basis of His sovereign will as part of His covenant purposes for the Jews and for mankind.

God's Covenant with Israel

Rabbi Abraham Joshua Heschel, a modern Jewish rabbi, has summarized what the land of Israel means to the Jews:

> The love of this land was due to an imperative, not an instinct, not a sentiment. There is a covenant, an engagement of the people to the land. We live by covenants," he wrote. "We should not betray our pledge or discard the promise. When Israel was driven into exile, the pledge became a prayer, the prayer became a dream, the dream became a passion, a duty, a dedication. It is a commitment

we must not betray. To abandon the land would be to make a mockery of all of our longings and our prayers and our commitments. To abandon the land would be to repudiate the Bible.[2]

There are two aspects of God's covenant with Abraham and his descendants: It was exact and it was everlasting.

1. God's covenant was an exact covenant

In Genesis 15:18 God spelled out the boundaries of the land He gave to Abraham: "From the river of Egypt to the great river, the River Euphrates." This is not spiritualized language. These are geographical references that were identifiable then and now. "Land" in the Old Testament doesn't mean "heaven" or some other spiritual dimension. It means *land*. And in this case, from the southeast corner of the Mediterranean Sea (around Kadesh; Ezekiel 47:19) to the Euphrates river in the east, and to just north of Damascus in the north. It was a clearly defined geographical area that was given by God to Abraham and his descendants (see Figure 1).

2. God's covenant was an everlasting covenant

Genesis 17:7–8 says the covenant would be not just with Abraham but his descendants "for an everlasting covenant." "Also," God said, "I give to you and your descendants after you the land in which you are a stranger, all the land of Canaan, as an everlasting possession; and I will be their God" (verse 8).

Israel does not now, nor has she ever, fully possessed all the land given to her. To do so today would mean Israel would occupy Israel, Lebanon, the West Bank of the Jordan, plus portions of Syria, Iraq, and Saudi Arabia. But it is hers and she will occupy it during the Millennium when Jesus rules from Jerusalem.

THE RELOCATION OF THE PEOPLE OF ISRAEL

Israel has only been back in the land as a nation since 1948 because of having been scattered across the face of the earth and suffering for centuries.

The Scattering of the Jewish People

The land of Israel has been overrun by the Gentiles since A.D. 70 except for very brief periods. Israel's disregard for her covenant obligations before God resulted in her being cast off the land at the hand of Gentile kings. This was part of the warning given to Israel that she ignored: "And the Lord will scatter you among the peoples, and you will be left few in number among the nations where the Lord will drive you" (Deuteronomy 4:27; see also Ezekiel 12:15 and Hosea 9:17). Israel failed to heed God's warning and spent 1,900 years removed from her promised homeland—until May 14, 1948 when the regathering of her people began.

The Suffering of the Jewish People

God also told Israel this: "And among those nations you shall find no rest, nor shall the sole of your foot have a resting place; but there the Lord will give you a trembling heart, failing eyes, and anguish of soul" (Deuteronomy 28:65). This quote from a documentary film about the suffering of the Jews summarizes their fate under the Nazi regime in Europe in the 1940s:

> Before and during World War II, Jews throughout Europe were the target of merciless state-sponsored persecution. In 1933, nine million Jews lived in twenty-one European countries. By 1945, two out of three European Jews had been murdered. When the smoke finally cleared, the terrible truth came out. The Holocaust brought about the extermination of one-third of the worldwide Jewish population at the time. Following the German invasion of the Soviet Union in 1941, mobile killing units following the German army began shooting massive numbers of Jews on the outskirts of conquered cities and towns. Seeking more efficient means to accomplish their obsession, the Nazis created a private and organized method of killing huge numbers of Jewish civilians. Extermination centers were established in Poland. Millions died in the ghettos and concentration camps through starvation, execution, brutality and disease. Of the six million Jews murdered during the Second World War, more than half were exterminated in the Nazi death camps. And the names Treblinka, Auschwitz, and Dachau became synonymous with the horrors of the Holocaust.[3]

To go through the two memorials in Jerusalem dedicated to the Holocaust victims—the Yad Vashem ("a memorial and a name") and the children's memorial—is a heart-wrenching experience. Few people make it through those memorial facilities without weeping, the presentation of the suffering of the Jews is so graphic.

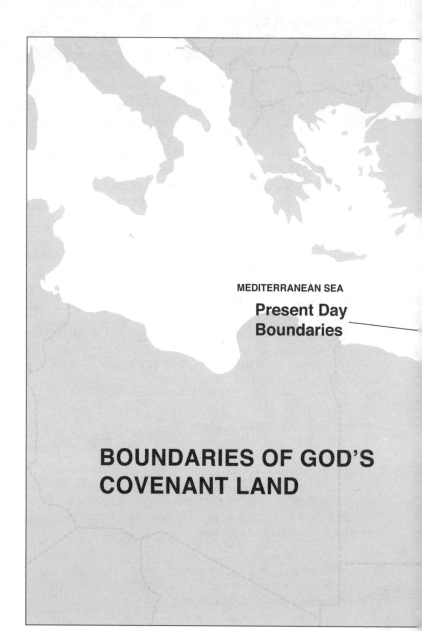

MEDITERRANEAN SEA

Present Day Boundaries

BOUNDARIES OF GOD'S COVENANT LAND

Figure 1

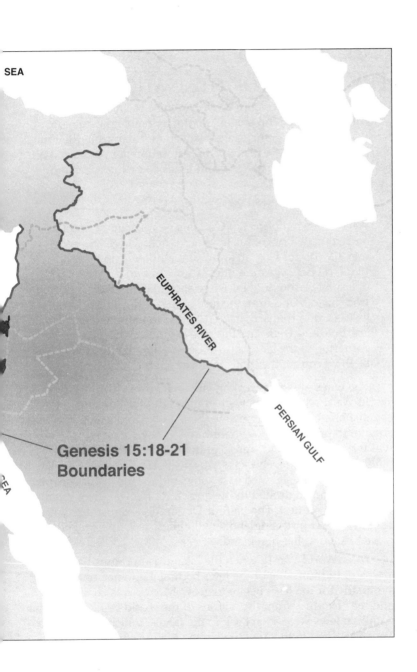

SEA

EUPHRATES RIVER

PERSIAN GULF

Genesis 15:18-21 Boundaries

SEA

Only the covenant promise of God has been sufficient to keep the Jews alive as a people today. Any other nation would have vanished off the earth (as most of Israel's ancient neighbor nations have).

THE REBIRTH OF THE NATION OF ISRAEL

Isaiah 11:11–12 contains God's promise to "recover the remnant of His people who are left . . . [to] assemble the outcasts of Israel and gather together the dispersed of Judah from the four corners of the earth." This hope of restoration has comforted believing Jews for 1,900 years, and it has come to pass in our lifetime.

Gary Frazier has written,

What an incredible act of God this is. You cannot find the ancient neighbors of the Jews anywhere. Have you ever met a Moabite? Do you know any Hittites? Are there any tours to visit the Ammonites? Can you find the postal code of a single Edomite? No! These ancient peoples disappeared from history and from the face of the earth. Yet the Jews, just as God promised, have returned to their land and they are alive and well. And they are beginning this final regathering to the land of promise which will ultimately be filled during the thousand year reign of Christ.[4]

The ways of God's working are mysterious. Toward the end of World War I when things were going badly for England, a Jewish chemist named Weizmann gave them a way to develop TNT fast enough to produce enough munitions to save the nation. When the war was over, England was so grateful to Weizmann that they offered him a "blank check," so to speak. He asked that the Palestinian lands be designated as a homeland for the Jewish people. Since England controlled those lands after the war, they granted Weizmann's request. The Balfour Declaration, signed on November 2, 1917, set forth England's willingness to help Israel be reestablished in her homeland.

After World War II, when the Nazi prison camps were liberated and the suffering of the Jews became known, a universal sympathy for the Jews began to grow. Money was contributed and the "exodus" from the nations of the world began. More than a million Jews were soon back in the land—which brings us to May 14, 1948. On that day the United Nations officially recognized the state of Israel with U. S. President Harry Truman determining the deciding vote. England left Palestine and the Jews were on their own.

The movement has been a political one—the Zionist movement—not a spiritual one. But her spiritual restoration is coming now that she is back in her homeland.

THE RETURN TO THE GOD OF ISRAEL

Ezekiel the prophet spelled out the spiritual return of Israel to her God in Ezekiel 36:24–28. God promised to give Israel a "new heart" and a "new spirit," to put His Spirit within her, cause her to walk in His statutes, and keep His judgments (see also Jeremiah 32:37–38).

There were 650,000 Jews in Israel by 1948—now there are more than five million, with six million expected by 2020. This regathering of the Jews is the precursor for all the end-time prophecies yet to be fulfilled. That single event assures us that we are living in the final days of God's plan—the time when Christ will come to rule over His people. It is amazing to me to live in the generation that has seen Israel's regathering. Throughout my father's ministry, he could not have had assurance that we were in the end-times since he ministered prior to 1948. I was born in 1941 and so have witnessed these events during my own ministry. It has made preaching and teaching the prophetic portions of Scripture that much more meaningful.

For Christians who are alive today, this should be an era of great urgency—one in which we redouble our efforts to get the Gospel of Jesus Christ to the world. If we understand the significance of God's promises to Abraham's descendants and the moving of those descendants back to their Promised Land, we will know that it is time to "look up and lift up [our] heads, because [our] redemption draws near" (Luke 21:28). I believe a great harvest of souls is going to begin in these final days as the return of Christ draws near.

For those who do not know the Lord, it is also the era of opportunity—the day of salvation. God has provided signs to alert the world that the end is drawing nigh. The invitation to be saved and to avoid the judgment to come is issued to all who have not accepted Christ as Savior. It is foolish to put off life's most important decision. The thought that time still remains to deliberate and make that decision is arrogant at the very least. No one knows what tomorrow holds—today might be the last opportunity that any person has to be saved.

If tomorrow is the day that Christ returns for His Church before the beginning of the Great Tribulation, will you be ready? If you don't know Christ, consider the magnitude of meaning found in Israel's return to her land. If God has fulfilled that prophecy, will He fail to fulfill all the others that remain? The world in which we live grows more and more perilous. But all of it is known to God. His plan for this world will be fulfilled, and that includes the promise that all who are found in Christ will inherit eternal life—and those who are not, won't.

So do not wait any longer. Call upon the name of the Lord Jesus Christ today in order that you might be assured of your salvation. Israel's re-birth date was May 14, 1948. There could not be a better new-birth date for you than today. God's promises to you—to all who belong to Him—will be just as sure as His promises to Israel.

Notes:

1. Gary Frazier, *Signs of the Coming of Christ* (Arlington: Discovery Ministries, 1998), 51–52.

2   Abraham Joshua Heschel, *Israel: An Echo of Eternity* (Woodstock: Jewish Lights Publishing, 1997), 57.

3. Joel C. Rosenberg, *Epicenter DVD* (Carol Stream: Tyndale House Publishers, Inc., 2007).

4. Gary Frazier, p. 67.

1. Read Genesis 12:1–3.

   a. Who did God choose in the beginning—Abraham or the Jews? (verse 1)

   b. In verse 2a God promised he would make a _____ _____ from Abraham.

   c. In verse 2b God promised to make Abraham's name _____ .

   d. The fate of all other nations would depend on what? (verse 3a)

   e. Can you give examples of nations and their fate, based on their treatment of Israel?

   f. What was the first promise God made concerning the land? (12:7)

   g. How many descendants did Abraham have? (Hebrews 11:12)

2. Read Deuteronomy 7:6–9.

   a. For what purpose did God choose Abraham and his descendants? (verse 6)

   b. Why did God rescue the Jews from slavery in Egypt? (verse 8)

c. What is meant by "a thousand generations?" Does the covenant God made with Abraham end after the thousandth generation? (verse 9)

d. What was the condition for the covenant being exercised toward any generation? (verse 9)

3. In spite of what reality did God bless the Jews with the gift of the Promised Land? (Deuteronomy 9:6)

a. What was their spiritual attitude even after being rescued from Egypt? (verse 7)

b. On the basis of what promise did God continue to bless them in spite of their lack of obedience?

4. Read Jeremiah 31:35–37 and describe what conditions would have to take place in order for God to disavow the covenant promises He made to Abraham and His descendants.

DID YOU KNOW?

When giving the boundaries of the land promised to Abraham and his descendants, God made reference to "the river of Egypt" (Genesis 15:18). The great river of Egypt is the Nile River, but it would be wrong to interpret "the river of Egypt" to be the Nile. The "river" spoken of by God was not actually a river but a wadi, or small valley, that flows with water during the winter rainy season but dries up during the summer. Most maps of Bible lands show this wadi, or brook, on the southern border of Judah's tribal territory, just west of Kadesh Barnea. It served as an unofficial boundary between Canaan and Egypt.

THE CRUDE AWAKENING

Luke 12:54–56

In this lesson we see how oil is beginning to shape end-time alliances in the Middle East.

OUTLINE

The majority of the world's known petroleum reserves are controlled by a group of nations who oppose Israel, some of whom oppose the United States. Strategic alliances may form around oil in the future and result in alignments that were predicted millennia ago in the pages of Scripture.

I. **The Control of the World's Oil Supply**

II. **The Consumers of the World's Oil Supply**

III. **The Conflicts Over the World's Oil Supply**

IV. **The Concerns About the World's Oil Supply**
   A. Are We Running Out of Oil?
   B. Can We Protect Our Sources of Oil?
   C. Is There Any Oil in Israel?
   D. How Does the Oil Situation Affect Our Future?
   E. How Then Shall We Live?

On August 27, 1859, Edward Drake launched the modern petroleum industry by drilling a 69.5-foot-deep oil well near Titusville, Pennsylvania—the first well dug for the purpose of extracting oil from the ground. Today, petroleum is the most valuable (most widely used) commodity in the world. The run-up in petroleum product prices in the United States beginning in 2007 has created an unprecedented economic disturbance—a crude awakening.

No one would have thought, 150 years ago, that petroleum would become a bargaining chip among the nations of the world. And prior to the discovery of the vast oil reserves in the Middle East, no one connected oil to end-time prophecies. But there is definitely a connection which is the subject of this lesson.

Jesus Christ once criticized the Jewish religious leaders for not being able to discern the signs of the times in which they lived (Luke 12:54–56). We might be deserving of that same criticism if we do not note the important role that oil is going to play in shaping geopolitical end-time events.

THE CONTROL OF THE WORLD'S OIL SUPPLY

Five of the top six nations with the largest proven oil reserves are Arab nations: Saudi Arabia, Iran, Iraq, Kuwait, and United Arab Emirates. The Unites States is number 11 on the list of nations. Saudi Arabia has around 265 billion barrels of oil while the U. S. has 21 billion. About 60 percent of the known oil reserves in the world lie beneath the sandy surface of Middle Eastern nations (see Figure 2).

While American oil companies were the ones who went to the Middle East to help those nations develop their petroleum industries, all the Middle Eastern oil is now nationalized— controlled by the governments of those nations. That means that 60 percent of the world's known oil reserves is in the grip of a very small number of powerful Arab rulers. Even the country that is number seven on the list, Venezuela, is no friend of the United States. The president of Venezuela, Hugo Chavez, has established alliances with Persian Gulf countries in opposition to the United States. So America finds itself in a precarious position when it comes to petroleum reserves. And students of biblical prophecy are seeing how end-times events will be concentrated in the Middle East because of the connection between petroleum and power.

THE CONSUMERS OF THE WORLD'S OIL SUPPLY

Here are the top four petroleum consuming countries in the world today, beginning with the biggest consumer: United States, the European Union, China, and Japan. And at the rate it is growing, it will not be long before China overtakes the European Union.

The United States consumes one-fourth of all the oil produced in the world. Remember: we are the eleventh largest holder of known reserves but the number one consumer of petroleum products. It is expected that America's oil consumption will rise to 34 percent of the world's output by 2030. And when it comes to gasoline consumption, America consumes 43 percent of the gas refined in the world today. And no new petroleum refinery has been built in America since 1976.

America's consumption of oil and gas compared with her holdings present a troubling picture. The search for alternative fuel sources for cars is under way with the most recent attention being given to ethanol. But it would take 97 percent of America's land mass to grow enough corn to produce enough ethanol for all America's cars—which would only create a massive food shortage. There is no immediate solution to America's petroleum dependence, which is part of the end-time picture.[1]

THE CONFLICTS OVER THE WORLD'S OIL SUPPLY

Arab unity, and ultimately Arab control of much of the world's petroleum supply, began when the Arab nations united against Israel in 1973 in what is now known as the Yom Kippur War. On October 17, 1973, those nations agreed together to reduce their oil supply to nations that favored Israel—primarily the United States and the Netherlands. The price of oil quadrupled in price to $12 a barrel (as of this writing it is over $130 a barrel) and lines formed at gas stations across America. For the first time, the unified Arab nations had an impact on the world economy.

In his State of the Union address on January 23, 1980, President Carter set forth what became known as the "Carter Doctrine"—that any nation's attempt to limit the free flow of oil through the Persian Gulf would be met by American resistance, to include military

TOP OIL RESERVES BY COUNT
*SEE CONVENTIONAL OIL RESERVES CHART

*CANADA

UNITED STATES
OF AMERICA (11)

ISRA

VENEZUELA (6)

Figure 2

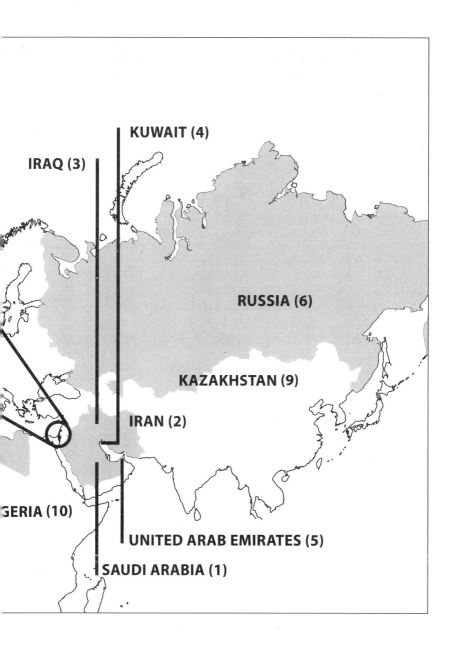

KUWAIT (4)

IRAQ (3)

RUSSIA (6)

KAZAKHSTAN (9)

IRAN (2)

GERIA (10)

UNITED ARAB EMIRATES (5)

SAUDI ARABIA (1)

force. When Iraq invaded Kuwait in 1990 in an attempt to take over Kuwait's oil supplies, President Bush implemented the Carter Doctrine and drove Iraq out of Kuwait to protect American interests in the Persian Gulf region. And then came the American invasion of Iraq in 2003 under the second President Bush following the terrorist attacks on America in October, 2001. The invasion of Iraq was about terrorism, but it was also about oil—deposing the ruler of Iraq who was the stated enemy of the United States.

As I prepare this study guide, the worldwide conflict over oil is as intense as it ever has been with no clear resolution in sight.

The Concerns About the World's Oil Supply

America's and Israel's interests in the world supply of oil are obvious given Arab control over so much of the world's reserves.

Are We Running Out of Oil?

According to some estimates, the world supply of oil is sufficient to power global economies at present rates of consumption for another 140 years. The problem is that we do not have access to all that oil—we are consuming oil faster than we are producing it. For example, in 2005, the world used more petroleum than was produced in 2006.[2] That is an unsustainable ratio—consuming more than is being produced.

Can We Protect Our Sources of Oil?

It appears that pure military might is not adequate to ensure an adequate supply of oil. Six years after invading Iraq, the price of oil per barrel is higher than at any time in history. Not even the most powerful nation on earth has been able to reign in the runaway cost of oil.

Is There Any Oil in Israel?

Former Israeli prime minister Golda Meir once quipped that, "Moses dragged us for forty years through to desert to bring us to the one place in the Middle East where there is no oil."

But that many not be true. At least two companies have been formed that are now exploring for oil in Israel based in part upon oblique references in the Old Testament. Ezekiel 36:11 suggests that God will "do better for [Israel] than at [her] beginnings." It is hard to imagine Israel being more prosperous than in the days of Solomon. But oil could be the key. Dr. Tim LaHaye has written,

"Suppose that a pool of oil greater than anything in Arabia were discovered by the Jews. This would change the course of history. Before long, Israel would be able independently to solve its economic woes, finance the resettlement of the Palestinians and supply housing for Jews and Arabs in the West Bank, East Bank, or anywhere else they might choose to live."[3]

John Brown, a Christian and the founder of Zion Oil and Gas, believes that Deuteronomy 33:24 and Genesis 49:22–26 indicate that oil is to be found in the area where the territories of the tribes of Asher and Manasseh met. In 2003, Zion Oil and Gas was given a license to explore 95,000 acres in that area. If oil is discovered in Israel it would change the entire geopolitical picture in the Middle East since Israel would no longer be dependent on Arab oil.

There have been numerous stories in major world media in the last several years on the search for oil in Israel. It hasn't been discovered yet, but that doesn't mean it won't be.

How Does the Oil Situation Affect Our Future?

Oil may turn out to be the commodity that shapes alliances between nations in the future.

1. The emergence of prophetic alliances

The prophet Ezekiel described a day when (what is now) Russia, along with Persia, Ethiopia, Libya, and others (Ezekiel 38:5), would attack Israel.

Until March 21, 1935, Persia was the official name of the country now known as Iran. To the best of my knowledge, not once in the last 2,500 years have Russia and Persia (Iran) been in an alliance—until now. Russia has signed an agreement to sell a billion dollars worth of military hardware to Iran, and Iran's nuclear scientists have been trained in Russia. The alliance foretold by Ezekiel is taking shape.

2. The emergence of petroleum alliances

Not only are there military and political alliances, there are petroleum alliances taking shape. I repeat: most of the world's oil supply is controlled by nations that are not friendly toward Israel. While some of the nations, like Saudi Arabia and Kuwait, value their relationship with the United States, it must be remembered that they are part of the Arab world. Their priorities and loyalties have yet to be tested.

A June 6, 2002, article in *The New York Times* quoted an Iranian religious leader who urged Arab nations to use oil as a weapon against the West and those who support Israel. He said, "If Islamic and Arab countries, for only one month, suspend the export of oil to Israel and its supporters, the world would be shaken."[4] It is clear that oil has become power and may become a powerful weapon in the future.

How Then Shall We Live?

It would be possible to look at the developing tensions among nations and the competition for petroleum resources, and grow discouraged. Living with the unknown in this arena behooves Christians to do three things.

1. Keep on waiting

In Matthew 24:32–34, Jesus used the fig tree as a metaphor for Israel, telling the disciples to watch for it to begin putting forth leaves. In other words, He encouraged them to be cognizant of what was happening around them as they waited for events to unfold.

We can apply that same lesson as we wait for the unfolding of the end times. We are waiting still, but our waiting is growing shorter. The growing tensions between the Arab world and Israel, and the Arab world and the West, are headed toward a climax. As individuals, we cannot impact those tensions. But we can wait with the confidence that God's purposes are going to be worked out. Jesus said, "But of that day and hour no one knows, not even the angels of heaven, but My Father only" (Matthew 24:36). We wait confidently while God's plans unfold.

2. Keep on working

Our task while we wait for the return of Christ is clear: to continue to labor in the Master's vineyard until His return. Many Christians throughout church history have made the mistake of supposing they knew the time of Christ's return and ceased from their labors. They have retreated from the world only to be disappointed when their expectations proved false. Jesus himself said, "I must work the works of Him who sent Me while it is day; the night is coming when no one can work" (John 9:4).

That must be our passion as well—to do the work of Christ while we have the opportunity. When night comes the opportunity will have passed. "Blessed is that servant whom his master, when he comes, will find [serving]" (Matthew 24:46).

What do you want to be found doing at the moment Jesus returns? When I was a boy growing up, our family had strict rules about things such as attending movies. Once when I snuck into the movies with some friends, all I could think about was, "I know the Lord is going to return while I'm in this theatre and I'm going to be caught!" Well, He didn't return then, obviously. But that story reinforces for me the idea that, in His absence and while awaiting His return, I need to be about His work. I want to be found to be a "good and faithful servant" when He returns.

Since we don't know the day or the hour of His return, it pays to be doing that for which we would not be ashamed every minute of the day. While we are waiting, we are to be working.

3. Keep watching

Finally, we are to keep watching—looking to the sky, as it were, for His return. In Luke 21:28 we find these words of Jesus: "Now when these things begin to happen, look up and lift up your heads, because your redemption draws near."

C. S. Lewis, in a sermon preached just before the Nazi attacks began on Britain, stated well the attitude Christians should have in times like ours: "This impending war has taught us some important things. Number one, life is short. Number two, the world is fragile. And number three, all of us are vulnerable. But we are here because this is our calling. Our lives are rooted not only in time but also in eternity and the life of learning humbly offered to God is its own reward."[5]

According to God's sovereign choice and plan, you and I are alive at this particular moment in history. We could have been born at any other time, but God saw fit to place us in the world here and now. And we are here for a purpose as we move toward the culmination of history on this planet. C. S. Lewis says it is our calling to be here when we are. But our lives are rooted not only in the here and now but in heaven as well—one foot in each, so to speak, suspended between heaven and earth as we await the return of Jesus Christ. Our ability to watch for His return without fear is based on the confidence that we have been called in God's kingdom for just "such a time as this" (Esther 4:14).

Vance Havner, the venerable Southern Baptist evangelist, wrote these words about the unsettled times we live in: "We are [not just] looking for something to happen: we are looking for someone to come! And when these things begin to come to pass, we are not to drop our heads in discouragement or shake our heads in despair, but rather, [we are to] lift our heads in delight."[6]

Are you watching with delight and expectation for His return? Sometimes we get so caught up in the affairs of this world that we secretly hope the Lord doesn't return today—not until we've taken that trip or gotten that promotion or made that purchase.

Dear friend, we are in the midst of a crude awakening concerning the world's oil supply. That will be the least of our worries if we are not found watching, working, and waiting when He returns. Better a "crude awakening" than a "rude awakening" when He appears!

Notes:

1. Figures on petroleum supply taken from John Walvoord and Mark Hitchcock, *Armageddon, Oil and Terror* (Carol Stream: Tyndale, 2007), 27.

2. Basic Petroleum Statistics (July, 2007 at www.eia.doe.gov/neic/quickfacts/quickoil.html. Accessed 10/2/07).

3. Tim LaHaye, *The Coming Peace in the Middle East* (Grand Rapids: Zondervan, 1984), 105.

4. "Mideast Turmoil: Tehran: Iranian Urges Muslims to Use Oil as a Weapon (*New York Times*, 4/6/02, at www.nytimes.com.

5. Timothy George, "Theology for an Age of Terror," *Christianity Today,* September 2006, p. 78.

6. Quoted in Calvin H. Fryar, *The Zero Hour* (Xulon Press, 2005), 24.

1. Read Luke 12:41–48.

   a. Who is the "master" and who is the "manager" (servant) in this parable?

   b. What is the servant's responsibility while the master is away? (verse 42)

   c. What is the Christian's responsibility today while awaiting the return of Christ? (verse 43)

   d. What will be the master's response to the servant who has been faithful? (verse 44; see also Matthew 25:21, 23)

   e. What would be the modern equivalent of the unfaithful servant's activity in the parable? (verse 45)

   f. What is the master's response to the unfaithful servant? (verse 46)

   g. Explain the relationship between what a Christian knows and what he is held responsible for by God. (verses 47–48)

   h. Based on what you know of the Master's will (verse 47), how does your activity in His absence correlate with His will?

i. How does the idea of the Christian's responsibility correlate with the talents in Matthew 25:14 and the idea of spiritual gifts in Romans 12:4 and 1 Corinthians 12:1?

j. Explain how verses 47–48 support the idea of proportional punishment or a proportional loss of rewards.

2. What did Jesus say about the time of His return? (Matthew 24:36)

a. What profound statement did Jesus make about His end-time prophetic words? (verse 35)

DID YOU KNOW?

Petroleum has traditionally been traded around the world in U. S. dollars, meaning that anyone who wanted to buy oil had to first exchange their currency for U. S. dollars. This has made the U. S. dollar the world's reserve currency, always in demand by oil buyers. Saudi Arabia's commitment several decades ago to sell its oil only for U. S. dollars has also provided stability. But that is changing. Saddam Hussein had begun a program to sell Iraq's oil in non-U. S. currencies (since reversed after the U. S. invasion), and Iran is now doing the same. If other countries follow suit, it could cause the U. S. dollar to lose value in international currency exchange since it would no longer be needed for oil purchases.

MODERN EUROPE . . . ANCIENT ROME

Daniel 2:31–45

In this lesson we track the modern revival of the ancient Roman Empire.

OUTLINE

The last great empire on earth, impacting the most people, was the Roman Empire (27 B.C.–A.D. 395). Since then, some leaders have tried and failed to rule the world. But the day is coming when a revived one-world empire will become the stage for the coming Antichrist.

I. **The Revelation of the Dream**

II. **The Interpretation of the Dream**
   A. The Kingdom of Gold: Babylon
   B. The Kingdom of Silver: Persia
   C. The Kingdom of Bronze: Greece
   D. The Kingdom of Iron: Rome
   E. The Kingdom of Iron/Clay: The Revived Roman Empire

III. **The Implication of the Dream**
   A. The Consolidation of World Powers
   B. The Coming of One World Leader
   C. The Condition for the Treaty with Israel

Two thousand, five hundred years ago a prophet of God stood in front of the most powerful ruler in the world and delivered a panoramic overview of world history—from his own time until the Second Coming of Israel's Messiah, Jesus Christ. Daniel was the prophet and Nebuchadnezzar was the Babylonian king.

Daniel's prophetic presentations were based on two dreams. One was a dream of Nebuchadnezzar that Daniel interpreted (Daniel 2) and the other was Daniel's own dream (Daniel 7). Both dreams had the same ultimate purpose: to communicate to the people of God the program of God for elevating His kingdom over all the kingdoms of earth.

The ten northern tribes of Israel had been taken captive to Assyria in 722 B.C., and the two southern tribes of Judah were taken captive to Babylon in stages in the late sixth century B.C. So it was easy for them to wonder: Is God finished with Israel? Do His chosen people have a future? Are God's promises made to Abraham still valid? Daniel's interpretations of the two dreams provided answers to those questions.

Nebuchadnezzar's dream was terrifying to him—so much so that he couldn't remember the content of the dream the next morning. When he threatened to kill all his wise men because they couldn't tell him his dream or its meaning, Daniel intervened and said he would reveal the king's dream and its meaning. Daniel and his three friends prayed to God for understanding and it was revealed to him (Daniel 2:17–23).

It is the interpretation of Nebuchadnezzar's dream that we will study in this lesson (Daniel 2:31–45).

THE REVELATION OF THE DREAM

The dream Nebuchadnezzar had was of an enormous statue that had five distinct sections (verses 31–33):

- Head of gold
- Breast and arms of silver
- Belly and thighs of bronze
- Legs of iron
- Feet of a mixture of iron and clay

The four metals—gold, silver, bronze, and iron—represented four distinct empires that would rule the world prior to the establishment of the kingdom of God under the rule of Christ.

THE INTERPRETATION OF THE DREAM

The dream is all about kingdoms (the word "kingdom" appears nine times in verses 37–44). A kingdom is the domain of a king; it represents the right to rule. In his prayer of thanks to God for revealing the dream of the king, Daniel said, "[God] removes kings and raises up kings" (verse 21). So God is the one who establishes kings and their kingdoms on earth. For all the posturing of men in elections and appointments, it is God who makes the ultimate decisions.

The Kingdom of Gold: Babylon

The first kingdom is Nebuchadnezzar's kingdom: "You are this head of gold" (verse 38). Nebuchadnezzar's kingdom began in 606 B.C. and lasted seventy years. Babylon was "dripping" with gold in terms of its wealth and was known in the ancient world as "the golden kingdom."

The Kingdom of Silver: Persia

The kingdom that followed Nebuchadnezzar's would be "inferior" (verse 39) to Babylon. It was Persia, represented by silver in the statue in Nebuchadnezzar's dream.

When Nebuchadnezzar's grandson, Belshazzar, succeeded his grandfather as king in Babylon, he hosted a banquet in which the God of Israel was mocked. A hand appeared on the wall writing out the fate of Babylon: "Your kingdom has been divided, and given to the Medes and Persians" (Daniel 5:28). That very night the Medes and Persians invaded Babylon and took over the realm. The two arms on the statue in Nebuchadnezzar's dream represented the Medes and the Persians.

The Kingdom of Bronze: Greece

In verse 39b, the third successive kingdom is mentioned—a kingdom of bronze "which shall rule over all the earth."

Greece was the kingdom of Philip of Macedon and his more famous son, Alexander the Great. Alexander extended the Greek empire over the known world: Macedonia, Asia Minor, the Middle East, north Africa, and Mesopotamia. It is said that he wept on one occasion because there were no more worlds for him to conquer.

The Kingdom of Iron: Rome

The fourth kingdom is noted in verse 40—a kingdom that "shall be as strong as iron, inasmuch as iron breaks in pieces and shatters everything." This fourth kingdom—the Roman Empire—conquered Greece and became the most dominant and influential kingdom in world history.

Rome assumed power in the Mediterranean world fifty years before the birth of Christ, and ruled Palestine through His ministry and throughout the expansion of the church in the apostolic era. The Roman influence spread further than any previous kingdom, throughout Europe and the British Isles. And they expanded ruthlessly—crushing all opponents with a heel of iron (see Figure 3).

The Kingdom of Iron/Clay: The Revived Roman Empire

The four kingdoms succeeded each other just as Nebuchadnezzar's dream predicted, one after the other. But the final aspect of the Roman Empire—the mixture of iron and clay—is the most important for us since it is still in the future (verse 41).

The ten toes on the feet of the statue represent ten divisions, or sections. Those divisions did not exist during the original days of the Roman Empire, so they remain for the future. And verse 44 says that at the time of this revived version of the Roman Empire "the God of heaven will set up a kingdom which shall never be destroyed." God's kingdom will "break in pieces and consume all these kingdoms, and it shall stand forever." That is the millennial kingdom of Jesus Christ which He will establish when He returns.

The original Roman Empire was not suddenly destroyed—it simply dissolved over a long period of time. So it will have to be reconstituted in a ten-fold form in the future in order for Daniel's prophecy about it being destroyed to come to pass. The process of a ten-fold Roman Empire being rebuilt is already under way. In 1946, in the aftermath of World War II, Winston Churchill said, "We must build a kind of United States of Europe." [1] In 1948 a conference was held in Brussels, Belgium, where the European Economic Community was formed. In 1957 the Treaty of Rome was signed which brought six European nations together into what was called the Common Market. In 1973 England, Ireland, and Denmark joined, and in 1981 Greece joined, bringing the total of nations to ten.

Some prophecy students thought that signaled the revived Roman Empire, but the text of Daniel refers to ten leaders, or powers, not necessarily ten nations. In 1986 Spain and Portugal were added and the European Economic Community adopted the goal of a political, unified Europe. In 1992 the economic borders between European nations were removed, making commerce and travel between member nations as seamless as traveling between states in America.

In 1995 Austria, Finland, and Sweden joined, and in 2002 the Euro currency was introduced. In recent years the Euro has gained value while the U. S. dollar has declined in value, illustrating the growing economic power of the unified European countries. When the Berlin Wall came down in 2004 and the impact of the dismantling of the former Soviet Union was realized, ten more nations joined, bringing the total to twenty-five, expanding the total European Union population to 450 million—much larger than the United States (304 million).

So there is now an economic and political union covering the same geographic area as the former Roman Empire—only much larger and stronger than before. This power needed to be in place before God's kingdom would appear and destroy it, making way for the millennial kingdom of Christ to be established (see Figure 4).

The feet of the statue were iron and clay. Iron represents strength, but clay represents the more subjective will of the people involved. It is a portent of the volatility of mixing power with people from so many different national and cultural backgrounds as has happened in the unified Europe of today.

THE IMPLICATION OF THE DREAM

So what does the dream mean in practical terms? How can we expect Nebuchadnezzar's dream to be played out in the future?

The Consolidation of World Power

In the days of the original Roman Empire there was one ruling power in the Western world: Rome. That has not been true since the dissolution of that empire. Hitler, Stalin, and others have tried but failed. But before Christ returns, world power will again be consolidated in one man. In the dream Daniel had (Daniel 7), which paralleled the dream of Nebuchadnezzar, Daniel was shown that "the ten horns are ten kings who shall arise from this kingdom. And another shall rise after them; he shall be different from the first ones, and shall subdue three kings" (verse 24).

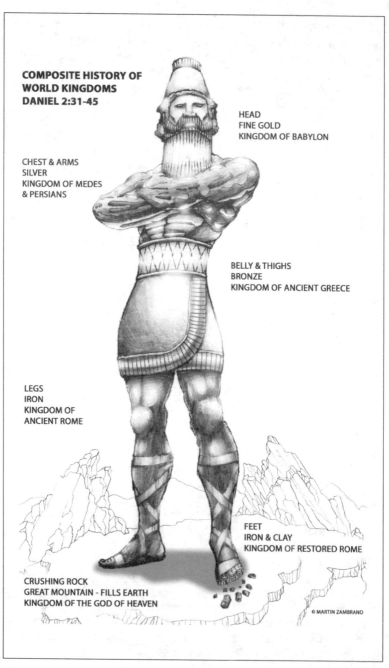

Figure 3

ROMAN EMPIRE
THEN & NOW

Old Roman Empire Outlined in Black
European Union Nations in Gray

FINLAND

SWEDEN

ESTONIA

LATVIA

LITHUANIA

DENMARK

IRELAND   ENGLAND   NETHERLANDS
LUXEMBOURG   POLAND
BELGIUM

GERMANY   CZECH

SLOVAKIA

AUSTRIA   HUNGARY

SLOVENIA

FRANCE   ITALY   ROMANIA

BULGARIA

SPAIN

PORTUGAL

GREECE

NORTHERN AFRICA   MALTA   CYPRUS

LIBYA   EGYPT

Figure 4

Modern Europe . . . Ancient Rome • 39

When I first began to teach on prophecy years ago, I wondered how one man could ever rule the world. As I have watched the confederation of European states come together in my lifetime, I now see that such an event is entirely possible. The "global village" that now exists through technology, communication, and commerce means that one individual's influence can be immediately transferred around the world. And to see nations who used to be enemies in Europe and the Mediterranean now joined together for purposes of commerce and protection—it suggests the possibility of one man rising to prominence over those unified nations. If world conditions—war, oil or food shortages, natural disasters—ever cause people to become desperate enough to give their allegiance to one leader he could easily become the ruler of a majority of the world's population.

The Coming of One World Leader

The individual that Daniel saw in his dream spoke "pompous words against the Most High" and "[persecuted] the saints of the Most High." He will "change times and law" and "the saints shall be given into his hand for a time and times and half a time" (verse 25).

We refer to this individual as the Antichrist (more about him in this study guide). He rises up as the leader of the revived Roman Empire and in opposition to the God of heaven and His people. In order for him to come on the world scene, there must be a confederation of states for him to lead, and that is exactly what is now in place in the union of European nations. Just a few decades ago, such a platform did not exist. But it is in place today—and the future leader of this revived empire may be alive in the world today.

Paul-Henri Spaak, the first president of the UN General Assembly, first president of the European Parliament, and onetime secretary general of NATO, is credited with making this stunning statement: "We do not want another committee. We have too many already. What we want is a man of sufficient stature to hold the allegiance of all people and to lift us up out of the economic morass into which we are sinking. Send us such a man, and, whether he be God or devil, we will receive him." [2]

While we may not be able to envision the circumstances in the future that would cause hundreds of millions of people to submit themselves to a "devil" of a man, the Scriptures say it will happen. The idea of interpreting Scripture on the basis of what we can or cannot imagine is a faulty idea. We must read what the Bible says about the future and then look for its fulfillment regardless of how implausible it may sound. Because the coming Great Tribulation is going to create a situation like nothing the world has even seen, we have to imagine the reality of people doing things to save themselves that they might otherwise never have done. And that includes submitting to a one-world ruler who promises to deliver them from the judgments of God.

The Condition for the Treaty with Israel

Daniel 9:26–27 tells us that "the prince who is to come" (the Antichrist) will "confirm a covenant" (treaty) with Israel for "one week" (seven years). So, the leader of the revived Roman Empire is going to establish a peace treaty with Israel for a period of seven years. That doesn't sound good—and it definitely will turn out not to be.

I'm sure you are aware of how much effort has been made in recent years to bring Jews and Arabs to the peace table. United States presidents Carter and Clinton both made strong efforts toward that end, and currently president Bush is doing the same. So it is not out of the question that the world's most significant ruler would be able to broker a peace agreement of some kind with Israel. Israel has even been willing to give up part of the land that is hers in order to achieve some sort of peace with her Arab neighbors.

However, the Antichrist's treaty will not last: "But in the middle of the week [the seven years] he shall bring an end to sacrifice and offering. And on the wing of abominations shall be one who makes desolate" (verse 27). The treaty will have allowed Israel to carry out her religious life under the banner of peace for three and one-half years. But the Antichrist will then break that treaty, signaling the countdown to Armageddon.

The way the stage is being set for these developments to play out, any objective observer would have to admit that the prophetic clock is ticking. Paul's words in Romans 13:11 are as true today as when he wrote them: ". . . now it is high time to awake out of sleep; for now our salvation is nearer than when we first believed." For us that means that the coming of Jesus is nearer today than it was for Paul; nearer today than when we were first saved; nearer today than it was yesterday. We may not know the day or the hour, but judging from Jesus' admonitions to judge the signs of the times, we ought to be able to know the season. And the signs certainly seem to indicate that we are nearing, or in, the season of His return.

Think of the things that have happened in the last 100 years. Israel was reestablished as a nation in 1948. There is in place a revived community of nations resembling the old Roman Empire.

The Arab nations control most of the world's petroleum which equals (in some important ways) most of the world's economic power. The wheels of commerce and the military are turned by oil. Is it not true that we have entered a different season? I believe it is the season of the Lord's return.

So the question is, Are you ready for this season? God's plans and purposes wait for no man. We need to either be in step with God's timetable or be left behind. The way to get in step with Him is to make sure you have committed your life to the Lord Jesus Christ, receiving forgiveness for your sins and the assurance of eternal life. If Christ returns today, will you be ready?

Notes:

1. William R. Clark, *Petrodollar Warfare: Oil, Iraq and the Future of the Dollar* (New Society Publishers, 2005), 198. W.S. Churchill, *Collected Essays of Winston Churchill, Vol. II* (London: Library of Imperial History, 1976), 176–186.

2. Paul-Henri Spaak, "Amazing United Nations Quotes," http://www.fdrs.org/united_nations_quotes.html.

1. Read Luke 19:11–12, 15a.

   a. What was the context of this parable? What were the people around Christ thinking? (verse 11)

   b. Analyze verse 12: Where did the nobleman have to go to receive his kingdom? Where did he go after receiving it?

   c. If a kingdom is geographical (a territory of a certain size), how did he bring the kingdom back with him? Therefore, what does it mean to "receive a kingdom"?

   d. Who does the nobleman represent in the parable?

   e. Describe Christ's going away to receive a kingdom, from whom He received it, and His return having received the right to rule.

   f. With regard to the Antichrist, who ultimately will allow him to have authority and rulership over men? (Daniel 2:21)

   g. But directly, who will give him authority and power to rule on earth? (1 John 5:19)

   h. Who will win the final contest for the right to rule? (Revelation 19:19–21)

2. What do you learn about Daniel's approach to the problem he faced in Daniel 2? (verse 18)

a. How did God respond to Daniel's humble approach? (verse 19)

b. How did Daniel respond to God's favor? (verses 20–23)

c. What distinction between man's ability and God's did Daniel draw in verses 27–28?

d. Who got the glory from Daniel's interpretation? (verses 30, 47)

3. Regarding the statue in Nebuchadnezzar's dream, how did Daniel explain the mixture of clay and iron in the feet? (Daniel 2:42–43)

a. How do you interpret "partly strong and partly fragile" in verse 42?

4. How ready are you for the arrival of the kingdom that will "stand forever"? (Daniel 2:44)

DID YOU KNOW?

The European Union (EU) at present has twenty-seven member states with a combined population of almost 500 million citizens. The EU generates approximately 30 percent of the world gross domestic product. There is a standardized system of laws covering commerce, travel, agriculture, and all affairs of the member nations. Twenty-three languages are spoken in the twenty-seven states. There is a motto ("United in diversity") and an anthem (Beethoven's version of Friedrich Schiller's *Ode to Joy*, in which Schiller expressed an idealized version of the human race united as brothers and sisters). There are currently thirteen currencies in use with the Euro being the most dominant.

(Above facts from Wikipedia article, "European Union.")

ISLAMIC TERRORISM

Ezekiel 38:1–6

In this lesson we are introduced to the fastest-growing religion in the world.

OUTLINE

The Muslim religion has existed for 1,500 years, yet it has only been in the last few decades that Westerners have become aware of the power and presence of Islam in the world. A minority of the world's Muslims are militant extremists for whom chaos is part of their life's mission.

I. **The History of Islam**

II. **The Habits of Islam**
   A. To Recite the "Shahadah"
   B. To Pray
   C. To Fast
   D. To Give Alms
   E. To Make the Pilgrimage to Mecca

III. **The Hatred of Islam**

IV. **The Hopes of Islam**
   A. Islam Hopes to Rule the World
   B. Islam Hopes to Return Their Messiah

V. **The "How To's" Regarding Islam**
   A. Do Not Compare Islam with Christianity
   B. Do Not Consider Allah as God
   C. Do Not Confuse Jihad with Salvation
   D. Do Not Connect the Qur'an with the Bible
   E. Do Not Conclude that all Muslims Will Be Lost

In a previous lesson we established the growing power of the Arab countries of the Middle East, most of whose citizens subscribe to the religion of Islam. But it is not just oil reserves that make the Arab-Islam countries a force to be considered. It is also because Islam is the fastest growing religion in the world. According to a 2007 poll conducted by the Pew Research Center, 58 percent of Americans know "not very much" or "nothing at all" about Islam. And regarding their perceptions of Islam, only 15 percent responded positively.[1]

In this lesson we will focus on the tenets of the Muslim religion so as to increase our awareness of this rapidly growing segment of the world's religious community.

THE HISTORY OF ISLAM

The word "Islam" means "submission" in Arabic. Therefore, a Muslim is "one who submits to god." Of the 1.3 billion Muslims in the world today, approximately four million live in the United States. The largest concentration of Muslims is not in the Middle East but in Asia.[2]

The founder of Islam, Muhammad, was born in Mecca (in present-day Saudi Arabia) in A.D. 570. His parents died when he was young, and he was raised by his paternal grandfather. He worked as a merchant until the age of twenty-six when he married a woman who was a wealthy, forty-year-old caravan owner. Together they had six children.

Muhammad was exposed to numerous religious influences in Mecca and, according to his own testimony, he received what he considered to be a divine revelation while meditating in a cave at age forty. The revelations continued throughout his life and were eventually compiled into what is now known as the Qur'an, regarded by Muslims as the word of god. There were more than 360 deities in the Arabic pantheon, and Muhammad chose the name of one of them, Allah, to be the true god.

As Muhammad's followers grew, they slaughtered everyone in their path who would not testify that "there is no god but Allah, and Muhammad is his messenger." Muhammad and his followers eventually fled to Medina where he became head of the first Muslim community in A.D. 631. Muhammad died the following year.

After his death the Islamic world splintered as the followers of Muhammad tried to choose his successor. Today, Sunni Arabs comprise about 90 percent of the Islamic world, believing that Muhammad's gifts died with him. For Sunnis the Qu'ran is their sole authority. (Saddam Hussein was a Sunni Arab, the minority branch of Islam in Iraq.)

The other major branch of Islam is the Shiites who identified with Muhammad's son-in-law after Muhammad's death. The Shiites believe that their leaders (imams) have spiritual authority equal to the Qur'an. They also believe that the Twelfth Imam was concealed hundreds of years ago but is still alive, to be one day revealed as the Muslim "Mahdi," or messiah.[3] The Sunni and Shiite Muslims today have a contentious relationship.

THE HABITS OF ISLAM

The primary practices of the Muslim faithful are referred to as the five pillars of Islam.

To Recite the "Shahadah"

The Shahadah is the Muslim creed: "There is no god but Allah, and Muhammad is his messenger." In prayer, Muslims repeat this prayer over and over almost as a mantra.

To Pray (Salat)

Muslims pray five times each day, the call to prayer wafting out across Arab cities from the local mosque. Muslims stop wherever they are at the moment and kneel down toward Mecca, first performing a ceremonial cleansing with water (or sand if water is unavailable). The prayers are memorized and recited in Arabic.

To Fast (Sawm)

The most important fasting time for Muslims is the month of Ramadan (September on the Gregorian calendar) during which they refrain from eating food during daylight hours. Ramadan is set aside for meditation and reflection and ends with a joyous celebration.

To Give Alms (Zakat)

Muslims are required to give 1/40th of their income to the poor and needy.

To Make the Pilgrimage to Mecca (Hajj)

The fifth pillar is the once-in-a-lifetime pilgrimage to Mecca, required of all who are physically and financially able. The journey usually takes at least one week and includes stops at many other Islamic holy sites along the way.

THE HATRED OF ISLAM

In the Middle East, we have seen Muslim extremists engage in all manner of violence. Indeed, America was the target of extremist violence and hatred on September 11, 2001. Associated with these attacks is the Arabic word "jihad," a word unknown to most of us in the West a decade ago. Jihad is often called the sixth pillar of Islam—it means "struggle." Spiritually, jihad refers to the struggle of the individual to submit to Allah, while outwardly it refers to defending the Muslim religion and culture. A big part of jihad is martyrdom, the culture of death. Martyrdom for the sake of Islam is considered a privilege and a great honor.

The Muslim hatred for Israel began in modern times in 1948 when Palestine was returned to Israel as a homeland. And because America is an ally of Israel, Americans have become targets of jihad as well (whether here, in Iraq, or Afghanistan). Experts believe that there are millions and millions of Muslims who are willing to die as martyrs to defeat their perceived enemies. Those who are violent extremists don't represent all of Islam, but they have given the religion and culture a bad name by their actions.

THE HOPES OF ISLAM

The hopes of Islam are some of the least known aspects of the religion to Westerners.

Islam Hopes to Rule the World

Radical Islamists have one ultimate goal: to cover the globe with the teachings of Muhammad and bring all into submission to Allah. The former Ayatollah Khomeini of Iran once said, "The governments of the world should know that Islam cannot be defeated. Islam will be victorious in all the countries of the world and Islam and the teaching of the Qur'an will prevail all over the world."[4] This doesn't always mean a violent jihad.

Islam Hopes to Return Their Messiah

In 2005 Iranian president Ahmadinejad spoke before the United Nations to explain his country's continued pursuit of nuclear technology. He opened his remarks with this prayer: "Oh Allah, the almighty and merciful, hasten the emergence of your last repository, the promised one, that perfect and pure human being. The one that will fill this world with justice and peace."

He was praying for the return of the twelfth Imam, a figure in Shiite Muslim teaching who parallels the Jewish Messiah in terms of significance. Because the Shiites believe the twelfth Imam will only return during a time of worldwide chaos, creating that chaos on earth is a way to hasten his return. This makes reasonable negotiations for international stability with a country like Iran out of the question since instability is what must precede the Imam's return.

Remember: Modern Iran is ancient Persia. The rise of radical Islam within Iran correlates perfectly with Ezekiel 38:1–6. There the prophet foretells an alliance between "Gog, of the land of Magog, the prince of Rosh, Meshech, and Tubal" and "Persia, Ethiopia, and Libya" plus "Gomer" and "Togarmah." Gog and Magog represent modern Russia. Never in history has there been an alliance between Russia and Persia—until now. Russia is providing extensive military and technological support to Iran. Ezekiel 38 foretells that this alliance will one day come against Israel and would completely overwhelm Israel without the intervention of God (which will happen).

From the Shiite Muslim perspective, creating chaos works to their advantage because it hastens the return of their Imam (messiah). What they don't realize is that the true Messiah will arrive at just the right moment to save Israel and destroy her enemies (Revelation 19:11).

THE "HOW TO'S" REGARDING ISLAM

This is not lightweight material—thoughts of international alliances leading to wars in the future can give any of us pause. And we must be careful as we think about the fastest-growing religion in the world. Here are five cautions when it comes to how to regard Islam.

Do Not Compare Islam with Christianity

Being a Muslim is not the same as being a Christian. Jesus Christ said that there was only one way to reach God the Father and that way was Him—Jesus (John 14:6). And there are many other differences:

- Christians do not call for the genocide of a particular race; radical Islam does (the Jews).
- Christians do not send suicide bombers to kill innocent people; radical Muslims do.

- Christians don't work for worldwide chaos to set the stage for the return of their Messiah; radical Shiite Muslims do.
- Christians work for the salvation of Muslims; Muslims call for jihad against those with whom they disagree.

So Christianity and Islam are not two different, parallel paths heading for the same place. They are different paths going in opposite directions.

Do Not Consider Allah as God

Allah is not God. Psalm 86:10 says, "You alone are God." They are not the same God under different names. Their character and teachings are so different that they could not be the same.

- Allah was chosen by Mohammad out of a pantheon of 360 Arabic deities; Jehovah God is eternal and self-revealing.
- Allah is not a trinitarian god; Jehovah God is Trinitarian: Father, Son, and Spirit.
- Allah did not die for man's sins; Jehovah God sent the Son of God to die for man's sins.
- Allah says, "Kill those who don't believe and you can come to heaven;" Jehovah God died for those who don't believe so they can go to heaven.

Do Not Confuse Jihad with Salvation

Salvation is totally different in Islam and Christianity. Titus 3:5 says it is "not by works of righteousness which we have done, but according to His mercy He saved us." Whether good works during Ramadan or through jihad, Islam is a works-based religion. Christianity is totally based on "grace through faith" (Ephesians 2:8–9).

Ergun Caner, a friend of mine and former Islamic follower who became a Christian, says, "Islam teaches that Allah's love and forgiveness is conditioned upon one's righteousness. The Bible teaches that God's love and forgiveness is unconditional, based not on how good one has been but on the death of Jesus. Salvation is not founded upon the enduring work of each person but on the finished work of Jesus Christ."

A converted PLO (Palestine Liberation Organization) bomber who came to Christ understands salvation and can explain it in his broken English better than most pastors I've heard! In Islam the only way to get to heaven is to die as an offering to God. In Christianity, Jesus Christ died in our place so we might go to heaven.

Do Not Connect the Qur'an with the Bible

The Qur'an is not "another Bible." Muslims believe that the Qur'an is the mother of all holy books and that the Bible is subservient to the Qur'an. But such a ranking is patently impossible! The Bible was written through divine inspiration by over forty authors over a period of 1,400 years with a consistent message from cover to cover. The Qur'an on the other hand, is a self-contradicting book supposedly given by the angel Gabriel to Muhammad. But since the latter could neither read nor write, the teachings of the Qur'an were translated and collected by those who heard Mohammad teach. Anyone who reads the Qur'an and then reads the Bible will find no similarity between them in terms of content and quality.

The last point may be the most important because it has to do with the work being done by the Spirit of God to get the Gospel into Muslim contexts—and the fruit that is being born. It would be possible to think that we are at a stand-off with the militant Muslim world, and to a degree that is true, for this reason: We have nothing they want. It is difficult to negotiate with people for whom negotiation produces no benefit. We have nothing to offer Islam except our souls since they want to cover the earth with the teachings of the Qur'an. And most Christians in the West—indeed, most people in the West—are not going to give up their beliefs or way of life.

So what do we do? We must remain strong: "Be strong in the Lord and in the power of His might" (Ephesians 6:10). We must maintain love toward those that hate us while, at the same time, we defend ourselves against theological error and compromise. And we continue to offer the Gospel of salvation to those who have not yet met the true Messiah, Jesus Christ.

The result is that the Gospel is making incredible inroads into the Muslim world. Our own Turning Point radio broadcasts, along with others, are heard in every Arabic-speaking country. We get letters from listeners in those countries who tell us what finding Christ has meant to them. And when they ask us to send materials to them, they warn against there being any indication that the materials are religious in nature as it could cost them their lives.

Do Not Conclude That All Muslims Will Be Lost

The promise in 2 Peter 3:9 certainly applies to Muslims just as it does to any other person: "The Lord is . . . not willing that any should perish but that all should come to repentance." We should never assume that any person or group of persons will be lost. Concerning Muslims, the evidence is certainly to the contrary: Many Muslims are embracing Jesus Christ as they encounter His Gospel.

I recently saw a bumper sticker on a car that said, "Have you prayed for Osama bin Laden today?" On an emotional level, we might recoil at the idea of praying for such a person. But Jesus Christ died for Osama bin Laden and for every militant Muslim terrorist just as He died for you and for me. In fact, it is for just such sinners as those who create havoc in the world that Christ died. Remember: "Those who are well have no need of a physician, but those who are sick" (Matthew 9:12). If you have a hard time hoping and praying that Osama bin Laden and Mahmoud Ahmadinejad will be saved—will become your brothers in Christ—then you need to remember that you were once the enemy of God as well until He reached out and brought you to himself (Colossians 1:21). Yes, we need to protect ourselves from our enemies. But we also need to pray that they will be reconciled to God through Christ. (And pray for the safety of Christian missionaries who are risking their lives to take the Gospel to Islamic populations.)

Two points in closing this lesson: First, do not fear what is happening in the world around us. And second, look up—the signs of the end of the age are indicating that our redemption is drawing nigh.

Notes:

1. "Public Expresses Mixed Views of Islam, Mormonism." Pew Research Center Publications. 9/25/07. www.pewresearch.org. Accessed 10/1/07

2. http://www.pluralism.org/resources/statistics/nimer_stats.php

3. Information on the history of Islam is from Winifred Corduan, *Pocket Guide to World Religions* (Downers Grove: InterVarsity Press, 2006).

4. Christopher Hugh Partridge, *Introduction to World Religions* (Minneapolis, MN: Fortress Press, 2005), 365.

APPLICATION

1. Answer the following questions from Genesis 16, 21, and 25.

   a. What was Sarah's solution to the problem of not having borne Abraham a son? (verse 16:2)

   b. What promise did the angel of the Lord make to Hagar when He found her in the desert? (verse 16:10)

   c. How is that similar to the promise God made to Abraham (and Sarah)? (Genesis 15:5)

   d. What was to be his (and his descendants') destiny? (verse 16:12—especially the last phrase)

   e. What did God eventually do for Abraham and Sarah? (verses 21:1–3)

f. From verses 16:3, 16 and 21:5, approximately how long did Abraham and Sarah have to wait before God fulfilled His promise to give them a son?

g. What was Ishmael's attitude toward his baby brother? (verse 21:9)

h. What did God say to Abraham about the two boys? (verses 21:12–13)

i. What promise did God confirm to Hagar? (verse 21:18)

j. What brought Isaac and Ishmael back together as adults? (verses 25:8–9)

k. How many sons did Ishmael have? (verses 25:13–16)

l. How many more sons did Abraham have after Sarah's death? (verses 25:1–2)

m. To whom did Abraham leave the bulk of his estate? (verse 25:5)

n. What was the ongoing relationship between Ishmael and his sons and Abraham's other sons? (verse 25:18)

o. How was the hostility between Sarah and Hagar played out in their children's lives?

p. Who became some of Israel's chief enemies? (Psalm 83:6)

q. Modern Arabs claim Ishmael as their forefather, and Jews are the descendants of Isaac. What modern hostility can be traced to Sarah and Abraham's impatience in having a male son?

2. What lesson about trusting God can you draw from the story of the birth of Ishmael?

DID YOU KNOW?

A July, 2007, *Newsweek* magazine survey of Americans revealed the following:

- 32 percent believe that American Muslims are less loyal to the United States

- 40 percent believe that American Muslims are as loyal to the United States as to Islam

- 63 percent believe that American Muslims do not condone violence

- 28 percent believe that the Koran condones violence

- 40 percent believe that the Koran does not condone violence

- 46 percent believe that America has too many Muslim immigrants.

Muslims make up approximately one-half of one percent of the American population.

VANISHED WITHOUT A TRACE

1 Thessalonians 4:13–18

In this lesson we study the doctrine of the Rapture of the church.

OUTLINE

Many Bible teachers avoid the prophetic portions of Scripture, citing their lack of practical relevance. But nothing could be more practical than the fact that Jesus Christ could appear at any moment to take His church to heaven. Preparing for that ingathering has eternal ramifications.

I. **The Careful Preview of the Rapture**
   A. Dispelling the Believer's Ignorance
   B. Describing the Believer's Death
   C. Defending the Believer's Hope

II. **The Certain Promise of the Rapture**

III. **The Chronological Program of the Rapture**
   A. There Will Be a Return
   B. There Will Be a Resurrection
   C. There Will Be a Rapture
   D. There Will Be a Reunion

IV. **The Comforting Purpose of the Rapture**

V. **The Conclusion of the Rapture**
   A. We Should Be Looking for the Lord
   B. We Should Be Living for the Lord

OVERVIEW

As I prepared the message on which this lesson is based, one million southern Californians were being evacuated from their homes and businesses in what became the largest enforced movement of people in California history. More than 350,000 homes were vacated as sixteen simultaneous wildfires swept through the area near where I live.[1]

I had titled the message I was preparing prior to the fires, calling it "The Great Disappearance." If I had known about the coming wildfires, I would have called it "The Great Evacuation." Regardless, the massive movement of people in southern California was a perfect way to contrast the mega-massive movement that is coming in the future. Millions of people from around the world will be "evacuated" from earth to heaven when the Lord Jesus Christ returns to gather His church, His bride, to himself.

Bruce Bickel and Stan Jantz provide a glimpse into how things will unfold on that day:

> Jumbo jets will plummet to the earth as they no longer have a pilot at their control. Driverless buses and trains and subways and cars will cause unimaginable disaster. Doctors and nurses will seem to abandon their patients in the middle of surgical operations, and patients themselves will vanish off of operating tables. Children will disappear from their beds. People run through the streets looking for missing family members who were there just a moment ago. And panic will grip every household, and every city, and every country.[2]

The event about which they wrote, and which we will study in this lesson, is the Rapture of the church. Before studying 1 Thessalonians 4:13–18, we need to clear up a point that has confused some. On the one hand, the return of Jesus for His church is imminent—meaning it could happen at any time: today, tomorrow, or the next day. On the other hand, there are many signs developing that point to His return. So how do developing signs fit with the imminent return of Christ? This diagram will help answer that question:

THE RAPTURE AND SECOND COMING

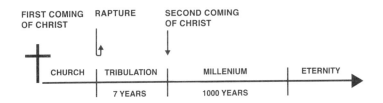

The key events leading to the Rapture of the church are Christ's birth, His death, resurrection, and ascension, and the birth of the church at Pentecost (Acts 2). We are living in the Church Age at present while Christ has returned to the Father in heaven. The Church Age will be ended at the Rapture of the church, which is why we say nothing remains that precedes that event. After the Rapture there are seven years of tribulation that are concluded by the Battle of Armageddon when Christ physically returns to earth, accompanied by believers who met Him at the Rapture. At the Rapture, Christ never touches earth (believers rise to meet Him in the air); but at the Battle of Armageddon, He physically returns to destroy the Antichrist and his armies. Then Christ establishes the Kingdom of God on earth for 1,000 years and the church reigns with Him. At the end of the thousand years, the Great White Throne Judgment takes place, and eternity begins in the new heavens and new earth.

Confusion about signs and Christ's imminent return occurs when people confuse the Rapture with the Second Coming. The Rapture of the church is imminent—there will be no signs preceding it. But there are signs that precede the Second Coming—the signs Jesus spoke of in Matthew 24. It is important to keep the two events separate and distinct. If we are already seeing signs for the Second Coming (and we are), that means the Rapture is at least seven years closer than the Second Coming! (See Figure 5.)

The promise made by Jesus to His disciples in John 14:1–3 ("I will come again and receive you unto Myself") will be fulfilled at the Rapture. It is an event known only to Christ and those who

Rapture / Translation	Second Coming Established Kingdom
1. Translation of all believers	1. No translation at all
2. Translated saints go to heaven	2. Translated saints return to earth
3. Earth not judged	3. Earth judged and righteousness established
4. Imminent, any moment, signless	4. Follows definite predicted signs, including tribulation
5. Not in the Old Testament	5. Predicted often in Old Testament
6. Believers only	6. Affects all humanity
7. Before the day of wrath	7. Concluding the day of wrath
8. No references to Satan	8. Satan bound
9. Christ comes *for* His own	9. Christ comes *with* His own
10. He comes in the *air*	10. He comes to the *earth*
11. He claims His bride	11. He comes with His bride
12. Only His own see Him	12. Every eye shall see Him
13. Tribulation begins	

Courtesy of Thomas Ice and Timothy Demy

Figure 5

belong to Him. The Second Coming, however, is totally different: "Every eye will see Him" (Revelation 1:7). The disciples did not understand the details of Jesus' promise, of course. Nor would we if we didn't have Paul's further explanation of these events in his epistles—1 Thessalonians 4 being the most detailed.

THE CAREFUL PREVIEW OF THE RAPTURE

Paul wrote to the Thessalonian church to clear up their confusion about the return of Christ, especially in light of the fact that some Christians in their midst had died without Jesus having returned. What about them? Paul assured them that those deceased saints would not miss out on the return of Christ.

Dispelling the Believer's Ignorance

The Thessalonians did not know about the stages of the return of Christ, and Paul did not "want [them] to be ignorant" (verse 13). Part of Paul's mission as an apostle was to teach doctrine that He had received from God (2 Corinthians 12:1–4; Galatians 1:17).

Unfortunately, there are many Christians today who are ignorant about the prophetic portions of God's plan—about when and how Christ will return for His church. Too many Christians, even many pastors, don't believe that what the Bible has to say about the future is relevant for today. As a result they live, like the Thessalonians, in ignorance of the knowledge and assurance these doctrines provide.

Describing the Believer's Death

Paul uses a comforting phrase to describe the members of the Thessalonian church who have died: "those who have fallen asleep" (verse 13). That is a New Testament metaphor for Christian death (Acts 13:36; 1 Corinthians 15:6, 18, 20; 2 Peter 3:4). It is the same metaphor Jesus used to describe Lazarus who had died: "Our friend Lazarus sleeps, but I go that I may wake him up" (John 11:11). It was also used to describe the death of Stephen, the first Christian martyr (Acts 7:60). It refers to the believer's body which is put into the ground on a temporary basis, waiting to be "awakened" by Christ when He returns for His church.

The Greek word for the burying place of the dead was *koimeterion*, from which we get our English word "cemetery." It was also used to describe a place where one would rest for the night, then continue his journey the next day. This is the same picture presented by "sleep" as a metaphor for death—it is the experience of one's body being temporarily buried in anticipation of being reunited with the spirit at the Rapture.

When a Christian loses a loved one who is also a Christian, there is mourning, of course—but not out of a sense of despair. For we know that the grave is only a temporary resting place for the believer's body (the believer's spirit is with the Lord) until it is raised again at the Rapture.

Defending the Believer's Hope

Paul did not want the Thessalonian believers to "sorrow as others who have no hope" (verse 13). Why? "For if we believe that Jesus died and rose again, even so God will bring with Him those who sleep in Jesus" (verse 14). If Christ was raised from the dead, it is not too difficult to imagine Him raising us from the dead as well. It was by the resurrection that Christ removed the sting from death (1 Corinthians 15:55–56). He proved that death is not final, and in doing so He created hope for us who also must die before being resurrected.

THE CERTAIN PROMISE OF THE RAPTURE

In verse 15 Paul answers the primary concern of the Thessalonians: What about our parents and others who have died? And Paul's answer is that "we who are alive and remain until the coming of the Lord will by no means precede those who are asleep." In other words, the deceased believers will go first at the Rapture! They will precede those "who are alive" when Christ comes for His church. This teaching would have given the Thessalonian believers comfort about their deceased loved ones, and it should do the same for you.

THE CHRONOLOGICAL PROGRAM OF THE RAPTURE

When the average person plans his day in the morning, they view it as reality—a plan of events that is definitely going to take place. Somehow, that same person—even a committed Christian—doesn't take the events that make up the Rapture with the same degree of certainty or seriousness. But we should. It's what the Bible says in plain language is going to happen.

There Will Be a Return

Verse 16 says it as plainly as it can be said: "For the Lord Himself will descend from heaven." He will return in the same way He left: personally (Acts 1:11). This is a very detailed statement by Paul, even including the sounds that will be heard: a shout, the voice of an archangel, and the sound of the "trumpet of God." I don't believe these are actually three separate sounds, but three ways of Paul describing a single sound that will be totally unique, unfamiliar to human beings. It will be the sound made by the return of Jesus for His church.

There Will Be a Resurrection

Paul continues in verse 16 to answer the Thessalonians' question: deceased saints' bodies will be resurrected from their graves. This is not a resurrection of all the human dead—that comes at the end of the Millennium when all unsaved humanity stands before God for the Great White Throne judgment. This resurrection is only those have died in faith prior to Christ's return.

There Will Be a Rapture

Verse 17 contains the heart of what is referred to as the Rapture: "Then we who are alive and remain shall be caught up." The word "rapture" comes from the word in the Latin Bible (Vulgate) used to translate the Greek word for "caught up." The English word "rapture" does not occur in the English Bible. This "catching up" is the same event Paul describes in 1 Corinthians 15:52—a change that happens in "the twinkling of an eye." That's not the "blinking" of an eye, but something even more instantaneous than that.

There have been other miraculous "translations" of individuals from earth to heaven. It happened to Enoch (Hebrews 11:5), Elijah (2 Kings 2:11), and the apostle Paul (2 Corinthians 12:2; though his visit to heaven was only temporary).

There Will Be a Reunion

The key word in verse 17 that indicates a reunion is "together." The first reunion is when the saints who are alive at the Rapture are reunited with those who have preceded them in death. Those who are alive will be caught up "together with [the resurrected ones]." The second reunion is when all believers—living and deceased—"meet the Lord in the air." From that reunion in the clouds, we all return together with the Lord to escape the coming Tribulation period on the earth (Revelation 3:10).

So that is the chronology of the Rapture: return, resurrection, rapture, and reunion. The result is that "we shall always be with the Lord" (verse 17).

The Comforting Purpose of the Rapture

In a postscript, Paul returns to the theme of this chapter: comfort for the believers in Thessalonica who had lost loved ones prior to Christ's return. "Therefore," he says, "comfort one another with these words" (verse 18). And the comfort they received from Paul's words can comfort us in the same way. When we stand around the casket of a loved one and later bury them in the earth, we are not saying good-bye forever. It is only a temporary absence. If we ourselves die before the Lord returns, we will join them in Paradise (Luke 23:43). And if we are alive when He returns, we will be reunited with them in the air when we meet Jesus face-to-face. I hope you will comfort yourself and others with these words.

The Conclusion of the Rapture

This doctrine of the return of Jesus Christ for His church should cause us to live differently in two respects: how we look toward the future and how we live today.

We Should Be Looking for the Lord

Many Christians don't know that the Bible specifically admonishes them to be on the lookout for the appearing of Jesus Christ: "We should live . . . looking for the blessed hope and glorious appearing of our great God and Savior Jesus Christ" (Titus 2:12–13). I can tell you this: The older one gets, the more he starts looking for the appearing of the Lord. Young people have too many other "priorities." But in the sunset seasons of life, making the transition to heaven begins to sound appealing!

Titus 2:12–13 wasn't written for "teenagers"—it was written for everyone who belongs to Jesus Christ. Keeping our eyes on the heavens is a way to keep them off the world. It is a way to "live soberly, righteously, and godly in the present age" (verse 12).

We Should Be Living for the Lord

It is at this point that I take exception with my pastor brothers who fail to find the practical relevance in prophecy. Nothing could be more relevant than living "soberly, righteously, and godly in the present age"!

The apostles Peter and John felt the same way. Regarding the "day of the Lord" (referring to another part of the prophetic calendar) Peter wrote, "What manner of persons ought you to be in holy conduct and godliness" (2 Peter 3:11)? Again he says, "Therefore, beloved, looking forward to these things, be diligent to be found by Him in peace, without spot and blameless" (verse 14).

And John wrote, "And now, little children, abide in Him, that when He appears, we may have confidence and not be ashamed before Him at His coming" (1 John 2:28). Also, "And everyone who has [the hope of seeing Jesus] in him purifies himself, just as He is pure" (1 John 3:2–3).

Think about it: If the Rapture could occur at any moment of any day going forward, is that not motivation for making every moment one that is pleasing to Him? Would you want to be found doing something carnal, shameful, or utterly sinful at the moment when that "shout," that "voice of an archangel," that "trumpet of God" is heard? At that very moment, "in the twinkling of an eye," you will be face-to-face with Jesus Christ. I believe if the average Christian would meditate on these truths on a daily, at least a regular, basis, his life would be different. Not only would we not choose to willfully sin; but in those unwitting moments of failure, we would confess them immediately and be restored to fellowship with Christ, prepared once again to meet Him in the air.

The most important way that prophecy changes our life, however, is by causing us to examine whether we are in Christ or not; whether we will participate in that coming reunion in the sky. If you have not placed your faith in Jesus Christ, do not delay. There is nothing preventing Him from coming for His own today. When He appears, you do not want to be among those left behind.

Notes:

1. "Firefighters Gain Ground as Santa Ana Winds Decrease." www.knbc.com 10.24.07. Accessed 10/26/07

2. Bruce Bickel and Stan Jantz. *Bible Prophecy, 101* (Minneapolis: Harvest House Publishers, 2004), 124.

1. Read 1 Thessalonians 4:13–15.

   a. What do people do who have lost loved ones apart from the Gospel? What do they lack? (verse 13)

   b. Who will accompany Jesus when He returns to remove from the earth those who are alive just prior to the Tribulation? (verse 14)

2. Based on verse 17, list the names of deceased Christians whose passing you grieve whom you know you will see again.

   a. If Jesus Christ returns during your lifetime, where will you see them next? (verse 17)

   b. How is your life different from those who "have no hope" when a loved one dies? How does your life reflect the truth of the Rapture? (verses 13, 18)

3. Read Titus 2:11–15.

   a. What was the first appearance of the "grace of God?" (verse 11)

   b. How does the first appearance of Christ give confidence to the idea of a second appearance? (verse 13)

   c. Why is verse 12, concerning behavior, placed between the two verses concerning Christ's first and second appearance? Why is His first appearance a motivation to prepare for His second appearance?

   d. What was the purpose of Christ's first appearance? (verse 14)

   e. How is verse 14 supported by Paul's teaching in Ephesians 5:15–27?

f. Is there any relationship or activity in your life today that you would not want to reveal if Christ returned today? What should you do to correct it? (Matthew 5:23–24; Ephesians 4:26; 1 John 1:9)

DID YOU KNOW?

The Latin word from which "rapture" comes is *rapio*—to seize or to snatch away. *Rapio* was used in the Latin Bible to translate the Greek *harpazo*, which has the same meaning: snatch, snatch away, catch up. The Greek word is used in Acts 8:39 to describe the Holy Spirit catching Philip away and taking him from Gaza to Caesarea and in 2 Corinthians 12:2–4 to describe Paul being caught up to heaven to receive revelation from God. Three views of the timing of the Rapture have been expressed in church history: Pretribulationism (it occurs before the seven year Tribulation), Midtribulationism (it occurs mid-way through the Tribulation), and Posttribulationism (it occurs at the end of the Tribulation). The vast majority of those believing in the premillennial return of Christ hold to the pretribulation rapture view.

IS AMERICA IN PROPHECY?

Selected Scriptures

In this lesson we examine the role of America in biblical prophecy.

OUTLINE

America's activities are scrutinized by the worldwide media on a daily basis. How is it that the world's most powerful nation is not mentioned in the Bible? We can identify reasons for America's blessings but only speculate about her role in the world in the prophetic future.

I. **The Sovereignty of God in the Founding of America**
   A. America Has Been the Force Behind World Missions
   B. America Has Been a Friend to the Jewish People
   C. America Has Been a Free Nation
   D. America Has Been Founded on God and His Word

II. **The Silence of the Bible on the Future of America**
   A. America Will Be Incorporated into the European Coalition
   B. America Will Be Invaded by Outside Forces
   C. America Will Be Infected with Moral Decay
   D. America Will Be Impotent Because of the Rapture

III. **The Spiritual Tensions Surrounding the End Times**
   A. The Tension Between the Material and the Spiritual
   B. The Tension Between Tomorrow and Today
   C. The Tension Between the International and the Individual

In the introduction to Peter Marshall and David Manuel's book, *The Light and the Glory,* they ask a very profound question: "What if Columbus' discovering of America had not been accidental at all? What if it were merely the opening curtain of an extraordinary drama? Did God have a special plan for America? What if He dealt with whole nations as He deals with individuals? What if, in particular, He had a plan for those He would bring to America; a plan which saw this Continent as a stage for a new chapter in the drama of mankind's redemption?" [1]

That question raises the subject of this lesson: What is the role of the United States of America in biblical prophecy?

THE SOVEREIGNTY OF GOD IN THE FOUNDING OF AMERICA

In retrospect, though America is nowhere mentioned in the Bible, it certainly seems that God has had a plan for this nation in redemptive history. America has been blessed beyond any nation on earth. Why? Why has America outstripped all previous civilizations in terms of wealth, technology, and other achievements? That doesn't mean America has been perfect. But it does mean America's blessings are undeniable.

America Has Been the Force Behind World Missions

One reason for God's blessing has been our involvement in world missions—taking the Gospel of Christ to the ends of the earth. America has provided approximately three-fourths of history's missionaries and the same amount of money and other resources. God blesses those who obey the Great Commission (Matthew 28:19–20) because He always blesses obedience. When 75 percent of the missionary activity in the world has emanated from a country with only five percent of the world's population, that is significant.

Following World War II, Americans started 1,800 missionary agencies and sent out over 350,000 missionaries.[2] Today, 95 percent of the world's population has access to some portion of the Bible in their language plus Christian radio, audio recordings, and other resources like the "Jesus" film.[3]

America Has Been a Friend to the Jewish People

America has also been blessed for being a friend to the Jewish people. God promised Abraham that He would bless those who blessed Abraham's descendants—and America has certainly done that. I have actually been accused by some of being a racist for singling out the Jewish people for special attention and favor. But I do that only because God does—He said the Jews would be His chosen people forever, the "apple of His eye" (Zechariah 2:8).

As long as Jews have been in America, they have been afforded the full rights of all citizens and the right to maintain their religious heritage. And since the reconstitution of Israel as a nation in 1948, America has been Israel's staunchest ally and protector. "I will bless those who bless [the Jews]," God said (Genesis 12:3).

America Has Been a Free Nation

America's commitment to freedom, since the writing of the founding documents, has been based on biblical truth. Christianity and personal freedom go hand in hand. The first thing dictators and totalitarian rulers do is remove religious liberty from the people. Because America has maintained her identity as the "land of the free" Christianity has been allowed full-expression. Jesus said the truth is what sets men free (John 8:32). And because America was founded by seekers of spiritual freedom the roots of personal freedom went deep into the soil of the new nation. Since its founding, immigrants have come from all over the world to live in America because they want the freedom and opportunity America offers.

In 2007 The Freedom House reported that 46 percent of the world's population lives in free to partly-free societies—which means that 54 percent do not.[4] America represents freedom to the rest of the world, including religious freedom. And God blesses freedom.

America Has Been Founded on God and His Word

Finally, America was founded and its government established by people who honored God and His Word. That was certainly true of the Pilgrim founders and the early colonists, and mostly true of the founding fathers. While it may be debatable whether America is presently a Christian nation, there is no doubt that it was founded as one.

George Washington said, "It is impossible to rightly govern the world without God and the Bible." Benjamin Franklin requested that each session of the Constitutional Convention be opened in prayer: "The longer I live, the more convincing proofs I see of the truth that God governs in the affairs of men." All one need do is visit Washington, D.C., and look at all the public buildings that have references to God inscribed on them—even on our coins, "In God We Trust." And sessions of Congress are still opened with a prayer.

Critics of Christianity can try to rewrite our nation's Christian heritage, but they will fail. History is history. America was established on God and His Word and has been blessed for it (Psalm 33:12; Proverbs 14:34).

THE SILENCE OF THE BIBLE ON THE FUTURE OF AMERICA

Most modern nations are not mentioned in the Bible unless they also have roots in antiquity (like Syria, Israel, Persia, and regions of Asia Minor and southern Europe). The United States is less than 250 years old so it is not surprising that the Bible is silent concerning it. We can say conclusively that the United States is not mentioned specifically in Scripture. This might seem puzzling since America is the world's superpower, and we are approaching the end of history when conflicts among nations are going to increase and a worldwide dictator, the Antichrist, will arise.

Here are several ideas that have been expressed concerning America's future in biblical prophecy.

America Will Be Incorporated into the European Coalition

Some believe that America will be incorporated into the revived Roman Empire (discussed in Lesson 3). The reason for this is that America, along with Europe, is considered "the West" as opposed to Middle Eastern and Eastern (Asian) nations. Culturally and historically, America is tied more to Europe than any other nations, so the thinking is that America might join with European nations in an alliance. I have already mentioned how the new currency of Europe, the Euro, is gaining value against the U.S. dollar. So perhaps Europe will strengthen and America will join with her in the future.

America Will Be Invaded by Outside Forces

Others have suggested that America will be invaded or otherwise weakened by an outside force. Several nations in the world besides America (not to mention terrorists) have nuclear capability, and others might acquire it in the future. America's financial condition has been so weakened by expenditures on wars in Iraq and Afghanistan and the soaring price of oil—who knows what might happen in the future.

A Harvard professor, D. Graham Allison, wrote a book called *Nuclear Terrorism* in which he postulates that a nuclear attack on America is more likely than not in the next ten years.[5] Polls have shown that a large number of Americans agree with that possibility. Only time will tell whether America is weakened by an outside force.

America Will Be Infected with Moral Decay

It has been well said that those who refuse to learn from history are doomed to repeat it. And what history tells us about the world's major civilizations is that most of them fell from internal weakness and decay, not from external conquerors. Or if they were conquered by invaders, they were so weak from moral decay that they could not mount a sustained defense. Babylon, Greece, Rome—empires that seemed invincible all gave way to greed and licentiousness. The average age of the world's great civilizations when they fell was 200 years. That means America is living on borrowed time.

The cycle of history in empires has gone something like this: they moved out of bondage to spiritual faith; from faith to courage; from courage to liberty; from liberty to abundance; from abundance to complacency; from complacency to apathy; from apathy to dependence; and from dependence back to bondage.[6] It is not hard to trace America's history on that path. I would say we have passed the midpoint and are somewhere in the second half of that cycle—which is a scary thing to contemplate.

If that which resulted in God's blessing in the early years of this county is given up out of apathy, can we expect God to continue His blessing? Here are three national sins that Scripture says result in God turning His back on a nation.

1. Ingratitude

Thirteen times Israel went through a four-fold cycle: rebellion, retribution, repentance, and restoration, as told in the book of

Judges. Later, when the prophet Jeremiah delivered God's warnings to the southern nation of Judah, he reminded them of how close they had been to the Lord in the infancy days of the nation (Jeremiah 2:1–2). Those were days of simple faith and obedience, of tender intimacy with the God of Israel—days long since abandoned by the nation. Jeremiah warns them that their idolatry was sure to incur God's judgment, and it did. America might listen to the same warning.

2. Idolatry

In verses 4–5 Jeremiah specifically accuses the nation of idolatry. In so many words, God asks the nation, "What have I done to make you worship other gods?"

Could God not ask the same question of America? Why would the most blessed nation on the face of the earth turn its back on God and worship the idols of greed, materialism, immorality, and self-interest? Gradually through the years we have pushed God out of the public square to the periphery of our nation's life. The farther away we push God from the center of our nation, the more His place is taken by chaos, factions, and economic struggles. We redouble our efforts and things only get worse. Why would we turn our back on the God who has blessed and protected us?

Former president Herbert Hoover spoke these words: "We have overworked the word 'new.' The practical thing, if we want to make the world over, is to try out the word 'old' for a while. Some old things made this country. Some old things are slipping and if they slip too far, the light will go out of America—old virtues, old religious faith, whole truth, integrity, honor in public office, economy in government, individual liberty, willingness to sacrifice. Our greatest danger is not from invasion by foreign armies. Rather our great danger is suicide by compliance with evil." [7]

Even the church of Jesus Christ in America has fallen prey to the temptation to invent "new" ways of doing things—only to find that the tried and true biblical patterns are best after all. If the church allows the culture to dictate how we "do" church we will fade into irrelevance. Our mandate for doing church comes from the Word of God, not the world. The Bible may be old, but it is one of the old things to which we need to return in the church and in our culture.

3. Indifference

Upon hearing Jeremiah's words, the people were indifferent (verses 6, 8). They didn't even bother to task, "Where is the Lord . . . ?"

They had become calloused, used to God's blessing. And they thought it would continue forever regardless of what they did. It's an attitude that is found in much of contemporary Christianity today: indifferent to the warnings of Scripture about becoming more friendly with the world than with God. Preachers are offering people words that make them feel good but which have no basis in Scripture. They are empty words of hope that vanish like the mist when the heat of tribulation bears down upon them. It may be a message of prosperity and success, but it leaves one spiritually bankrupt when life's difficulties come on the scene.

The final reason that America may have little impact on end-time events is actually a positive reason.

America Will Be Impotent Because of the Rapture

If the Rapture of the Church happened today and all true believers in Christ in America disappeared off the earth, approximately 25 million citizens (or more)—Christians and their small children—would vanish. Not only would America lose a large portion of her population but she would lose the best of her population: the salt and light that has been preserving the nation's spiritual strength. If America lost her most faithful and patriotic citizens, she would be in no position to play a major role in end-time events. That may well be why America plays no significant role in the last days of planet earth: the best of her citizens have been taken to heaven.

THE SPIRITUAL TENSIONS SURROUNDING THE END-TIME

There is always tension in spiritual truth, and end-times prophecy is no exception. We need to be aware of the following three realities as the history of the world draws to a close.

The Tension Between the Material and the Spiritual

We have looked at many material aspects of our world so far: nations, leaders, petroleum, money, and others. And they are important. But as in all aspects of life, the material has to be balanced with the spiritual.

The Bible is clear that life in this era is a spiritual battle, a holy war. In the final analysis, the movements of men and material on the earth represent spiritual dynamics going on behind the scenes.

The words of Zechariah 4:6 tell the final tale: " 'Not by might nor by power, but by My Spirit,' says the Lord of hosts."

The Tension Between Tomorrow and Today

When we study prophecy, there is the possibility of becoming so heavenly-minded (focused on tomorrow) that we are no earthly good (responsible for today). If we know all about the ten toes on Nebuchadnezzar's statue (Daniel 2) but are oblivious to the needs of our neighbor, then we have become like the Pharisees—making religion more important than people. To paraphrase Jesus' words about the Sabbath (Mark 2:27), "Man was not made for prophecy, but prophecy was made for man."

God's plans for the future will be fulfilled, but He has plans for us individually that it is our responsibility to fulfill today.

The Tension Between the International and the Individual

It is so easy for us to sit back and be critical of nations and leaders—especially our own. This calls to mind Jesus' words about removing the plank from our own eye before we point out the speck in a brother's eye (Luke 6:41–42). The Bible wasn't written for nations; "nations" can't read God's Word and respond to it. Only individuals can do that. If nations change and do the right thing, it is only because individuals choose to obey God and make their voices heard and their actions seen.

We don't know the prophetic future of America, but we do know the future of Americans. As individuals, we must choose to obey God today.

Notes:

1. Peter Marshall and David Manuel, *The Light and the Glory* (Old Tappan: Revell, 1977), 17–18.

2. Gordon Robertson, "Into All the World." www.cbn.com. Accessed 11/1/07.

3. Luis Bush. "Where Are We Now?" www.missionfrontiers.org. 2003. Accessed 11/1/07.

4. "The Worst of the Worst: The World's Most Repressive Societies." April 2007. www.freedomhouse.org. Accessed 11/1/07.

5. Graham Allison, *Nuclear Terrorism: The Ultimate Preventable Catastrophe* (New York: Owl Books, 2004), 14.

6. Alexander Fraser Tytler in John Walvoord and Mark Hitchcock. *Armageddon, Oil and Terror* (Carol Stream: Tyndale House, 2007), 65.

7. Herbert C. Hoover, *Current History* (Philadelphia: Events Publishing Company, October 1951), 256.

1. Read Psalm 33:8–22.

   a. Whose counsel ultimately directs the paths of world history? (verse 11)

   b. From what you have learned so far, how has God used America and England, two nations with a Christian heritage, to shape the future of Israel?

   c. When God is the Lord of a nation, what is the state of that nation? (verse 12a)

   d. Specifically, what nation is referred to here? (verse 12b)

   e. Could the promise of blessedness apply to any nation that makes God their Lord? Why or why not?

   f. What picture of God's dealing with men and nations is portrayed in verses 13–15?

   g. Of what ultimate strength are kings and armies in shaping the future? (verses 16–17)

   h. To whom does God pay special attention? (verses 18–19)

i. As far as America's future is concerned, what should be our attitude? (verses 20–21)

j. If mercy is God withholding punishment that is deserved, what reasons does America have to pray for God's mercy? (verse 22)

2. As a Christian, what traits in America do you believe God continues to bless?

3. How could America best apply Jesus' teachings in Luke 6:39–42 in international relations?

4. What is the best way for a nation to become a light to other nations? (Matthew 5:14–16)

DID YOU KNOW?

While many of America's founding fathers were committed to the integrity of the Bible, Thomas Jefferson was not. He created a book called *The Life and Morals of Jesus of Nazareth,* or *The Jefferson Bible* as it has come to be known. He took copies of Matthew, Mark, Luke, and John and cut out all the words spoken by Jesus himself and pasted them onto pages in chronological order to obtain a code of morals and ethics based purely on the words of Jesus. He did not trust the records of the four evangelists—how they interpreted or presented Jesus' words and ministry. Jefferson didn't publish the book in his lifetime, but it was published by the National Museum in Washington in 1895.

WHEN ONE MAN RULES THE WORLD

Selected Scriptures

*In this lesson we meet the man
who will unleash hell on earth.*

OUTLINE

History is full of the names of infamous tyrants who brutalized people for their own gain. Modern memory is scarred by the likes of Hitler. But a man is coming in the future who will make the brutes of the past seem tame. He is the opposite of Jesus Christ: the Antichrist.

I. The Personality of the Coming World Ruler
  A. He Will Be a Charismatic Leader
  B. He Will Be a Cunning Leader
  C. He Will Be a Cultic Leader
  D. He Will Be a Cruel Leader

II. The Profile of the Coming World Ruler
  A. His Inconspicuous Profile
  B. His Intimidating Presence

III. The Program of the Coming World Ruler

When I first began to preach the Bible in full-time ministry, I never shied away from the prophetic portions. I gave them equal time and emphasis as part of the "whole counsel of God" (Acts 20:27). But I do have a secret confession to make: Forty years ago I could not imagine how one individual could rise to such a place of prominence and power as the Bible ascribes to the coming Antichrist. We didn't think of the world as a "global village" at that time in history. But today the world is "shrinking"—we are connected by money, media, missiles, and materials as never before. Today, the idea of a one-world ruler seems totally plausible and becomes more so every day.

The crisis events of the end-times—not the least of which will be the instantaneous disappearance of hundreds of millions of Christians from around the world at the Rapture of the Church— will create an environment ripe for a charismatic individual to step forward and lead the world to a place of momentary stability. That man will be the Antichrist—Satan's superman. Instead of saving the world, he will lead it to the final battle of history, the Battle of Armageddon, where he and his forces will be defeated by the returning King of Kings, Jesus Christ. But prior to that time, he will demonstrate super-human (supernatural) powers such as the world has never seen (except in Jesus).

The Antichrist is mentioned in Scripture by way of several aliases: "the prince that shall come" (Daniel 9:26 KJV), "a king of fierce countenance" (Daniel 8:23 KJV), "a master of intrigue" (Daniel 8:23 NIV), "a despicable man" (Daniel 11:21 NLT), "this worthless shepherd" (Zechariah 11:16, 17 NLT), "the man of destruction" (2 Thessalonians 2:3 GOD'S WORD), "the man of lawlessness" (2 Thessalonians 2:3 NIV), "this evil man" (2 Thessalonians 2:9 NLT), "the beast" (Revelation 13:2 NIV), and, of course, "the Antichrist" (1 John 2:18; 4:3).

Based on the number "666" in Revelation 13:18, many attempts have been made in history to identify who the Antichrist is or will be. Using a system of numerology where letters of the alphabet are assigned numerical values, attempts have been made to find the names of historical figures the letters of whose names add up to 666. Surprisingly, many names have qualified mathematically. The only problem is that none have turned out to be the Antichrist.

The Bible does not tell us who the Antichrist will be— name, nationality, or any other specifics. In fact, Paul writes in

2 Thessalonians 2 that this coming world leader will not be revealed until after the Rapture of the church (verse 3). So if you are here when the Antichrist is revealed, you will have been left behind by the Rapture.

THE PERSONALITY OF THE COMING WORLD RULER

We may not know who this world leader will be, but we do know what he will be: charismatic, cunning, cultish, and cruel.

He Will Be a Charismatic Leader

Three times in Daniel 7 we are told that this man will speak "pompous words" ("boastful words" in some other translations; verses 8, 20, 25). In Revelation 13:5 we are told that "he was given a mouth speaking great things and blasphemies." He will be one of the most powerful orators the world has ever known and will use that skill to sway masses of people in the direction he wants them to go. Here is a description written by Charles Colson of a similar power possessed by Nazi dictator Adolf Hitler:

> Solemn, symphonic music began the set up. The music then stopped. A hush prevailed and a patriotic anthem began. And from the back, walking slowly down the wide central aisle strutted Hitler. Finally the führer himself rises to speak, beginning in a low velvet voice which makes the audience unconsciously lean forward to hear. He begins to speak of his love for Germany and gradually his pitch increases and increases until he reaches a screaming crescendo, but his audience does not mind because they are all standing on their feet and screaming with him.[1]

Anyone who has ever seen documentary film footage of Hitler speaking in those pre-World War II rallies in Germany knows the scene—and has experienced the chills of fear in watching a human being exercise that kind of power over people. Whereas Hitler had the power to captivate a nation, the Antichrist will have power to captivate the whole world.

He Will Be a Cunning Leader

Daniel 7:8 reveals another aspect of his ability: "I was considering the horns, and there was another horn, a little one, coming up among them, before whom three of the first horns were plucked out by the roots." Substitute "kings" for "horns" and you'll have an idea of the Antichrist's power to elevate himself by destroying others. He deposes three kings as he claws his way to power in that part of the world until he ultimately controls the whole Western world. Here's another view of his ability: "But he shall come in peaceably, and seize the kingdom by intrigue" (Daniel 11:21). Intrigue and cunning—the traits of a person who is the opposite of the true Christ.

He Will Be a Cultic Leader

He will demonstrate a religious-like fervor to attract followers to himself and away from God: "He shall speak pompous words against the Most High, shall persecute the saints of the Most High, and shall intend to change times and law." He will "[oppose] and [exalt] himself above all that is called God or that is worshipped, so that he sits as God in the temple of God, showing himself that he is God" (2 Thessalonians 2:4).

And he will be successful: "All who dwell on the earth will worship him, whose names have not been written in the Book of Life" (Revelation 13:8).

He Will Be a Cruel Leader

This ruler will "devour the whole earth, and trample it and break in pieces" (Daniel 7:23). He will spare no one in his quest for world domination. Believers will be absent from the earth due to the Rapture when the Antichrist's wrath reaches its peak, but he will persecute those who seek to follow Christ during the Tribulation. Many who become Christians during the Tribulation will be martyred for their faith. Most others will simply be worn down (the literal meaning of "persecute" in this context) by the Antichrist's relentless persecution and oppression of their faith. In much the same way that Hitler drove Jews to madness in the concentration camps, so believers will be worn down by the cruelty of the Antichrist.

THE PROFILE OF THE COMING WORLD LEADER

We are given enough information about this evil world leader to piece together a profile of his life and work for the few years he will be on the world stage.

His Inconspicuous Profile

We have evidence relating to his political, national, spiritual, and "providential" life.

1. Politically

Revelation 13:1 pictures the beast "rising up out of the sea"—the sea being a picture of the masses of humanity on planet earth (see a similar reference to "the waters" in Revelation 17:15). So the Antichrist does not burst on the scene. He rises slowly out of the Gentile nations of the earth, the nations of the revived Roman Empire in Europe, and gradually assumes power.

2. Nationally

The Bible doesn't tell us the nationality of the Antichrist. Some have thought he would be a Jew since he makes a treaty with the Jewish people (Daniel 9:27), but that is not a necessity. His charisma and cunning will allow him to forge political treaties and alliances with anyone. The best we can say is that he will come from among the ten rulers of the revived Roman Empire (the ten toes of Nebuchadnezzar's image).

3. Spiritually

His spiritual origin and empowerment is from "the bottomless pit" (Revelation 11:7). In short, the Antichrist comes from hell. The true Christ came from heaven, empowered by the Holy Spirit. The Antichrist comes from hell, empowered by Satan.

4. Providentially

Though this man seems to run amok, wreaking havoc on the world stage, he is on a leash that is tethered firmly in heaven. Note the words of Revelation 13:5: "And he was given a mouth speaking great things and blasphemies, and he was given authority to continue for forty-two months." Who gives him this authority to speak and to rule? God Almighty does.

It might seem that God is looking the other way during the period that the Antichrist rules over earth, but nothing could be further from the truth. Like every person who has ever lived, the Antichrist has nothing that did not come from God—and that includes permission to carry out his evil deeds. God does not give up control over His creation or His plans, and no one can wrest it from Him.

THE PROGRAM OF THE COMING WORLD RULER

Keep Revelation 13:2–3 in mind as we talk about the program of the Antichrist: "Now the beast which I saw was like a leopard, his feet were like the feet of a bear, his mouth like the mouth of a lion. The dragon gave him his power, his throne, and great authority. And I saw one of his heads that had been mortally wounded, and his deadly wound was healed. And all the world marveled and followed the beast."

The world is going to be looking for someone who can bring peace and stability to the Middle East. Remember that the majority of the world's petroleum reserves are there, plus the ongoing tensions between Israel and her neighbors. The Antichrist will come on the scene and be the savior. He will make a treaty with Israel on behalf of the nations. For three and one-half years there will be peace in the Middle East—until the Antichrist breaks the treaty and begins to persecute Israel.

At that point the Antichrist will be assassinated—I believe he will be shot in the head—but by the power of Satan he will come back to life in a veiled counterfeit of the resurrection of Jesus Christ. This prophecy reminds me of the day president John F. Kennedy was assassinated in Dallas, Texas, where I was a seminary student at the time. Can you imagine what the world would have thought if, in just a matter of hours, he had risen from the dead and began to speak? Imagine the reaction on the world stage when the Antichrist does just that!

Whether his death and resurrection is real or feigned, the world will throw their support to one as powerful as he. His lieutenant, the biblical False Prophet (Revelation 16:13; 19:20; 20:10), will establish a form of registration that causes all to receive "the mark of the beast" (Revelation 16:2; 19:20). Those who receive the mark will be able to buy and sell while those who refuse will suffer starvation.

The Antichrist will set himself up as the one to be worshipped in the temple of the Jews in Jerusalem, thus beginning his full-fledged attack upon Israel. Before he carries out that mission, Jesus Christ returns from heaven with His army of the saints who were raptured seven years earlier. The Antichrist is defeated, the Jews are saved, unbelievers from all history are judged, and the kingdom of God is established upon earth for a thousand years (Revelation 20:1–3).

If you think this sounds impossible, read this very possible-sounding description by Gary Frazier:

> Somewhere at this very moment, there may be a young
> man growing to maturity. He is in all likelihood, a brood-

ing, thoughtful young man. Inside his heart there is this hellish rage. He boils like a cauldron of molten steel. He hates God. He despises Jesus Christ. He detests the Church. In his mind, there is taking the shape of this dream of conquest. He presents himself as a friend of Christ in the church. Yet beneath his veneer of civility is a Trojan horse. He will, once empowered, pour all hell loose on this world. We ask ourselves, "Can this world produce such a person?" Hitler was a little boy one time. Stalin was once a lad. Nero was a child. And the tenderness of childhood will be shaped by the devil into the terror of the Antichrist.[2]

This person could be alive today as a child or young man—or a mature adult waiting to step into his appointed role. But that does not mean we will be here when he rules. The church of Jesus Christ (all true believers) will have been removed at the Rapture when his reign of terror begins. Therefore, Christians are not looking for the coming of Antichrist but the coming of Christ! Here's an acrostic version of what it means to focus on Jesus instead of the Judas who is to come:

A : We abhor the Antichrist, we adore the Christ.

B : We blame the Antichrist, we believe in the Christ.

C : We curse the Antichrist, we confess the Christ.

D : We despise the Antichrist, we desire Christ.

E : We explain the Antichrist, we exalt the Christ.

F : We fear the Antichrist, we fellowship with Christ.

G : We glare at the Antichrist, we gaze at Christ.

H : We hate the Antichrist, we honor Christ.

I : We investigate the Antichrist, we insist on Christ.

J : We judge the Antichrist, we are judged by Christ.

K : We know about the Antichrist, but we know Christ.

L : We loathe the Antichrist, but we love Christ.

M: We minimize the Antichrist, we magnify Christ.

N : We nullify the Antichrist, we need Christ.

O : We oppose the Antichrist, we obey Christ.

P : We put down the Antichrist, we praise Christ.

Q : We question the Antichrist, we quote Christ.

R : We reject the Antichrist, we reverence Christ.

S : We survey the Antichrist, we serve Christ.

T : We test the Antichrist, we trust Christ.

U : We unmask the Antichrist, we uplift Christ.

V : We vilify the Antichrist, we verify the Christ.

W: We warn against the Antichrist, we worship the Christ.

Y : We yawn at the Antichrist, we yearn for the Christ.

Z : We zone out the Antichrist, we zero in on Christ.

That's a playful look at a serious subject. We do not fear the Antichrist, and that is not just because we will be absent during His rule. Instead we fear (adore and reverence) the King of Kings who is coming to defeat him and save God's chosen people, the Jews, from annihilation. The book of Revelation is not about the revelation (appearing) of the Antichrist, but the Christ (Revelation 1:1). Knees may bow temporarily to the Antichrist, but when he becomes a defeated foe, the prophecy of Philippians 2:10–11 will be fulfilled: "That at the name of Jesus every knee should bow, of those in heaven, and of those on earth, and of those under the earth, and that every tongue should confess that Jesus Christ is Lord, to the glory of God the Father."

How much better to bow before Him now in praise and adoration!

Notes:

1. Charles Colson, *Kingdoms in Conflict* (Grand Rapids: Zondervan, copublished William Morrow, 1987), 129–130.

2. Gary Frazier, *Signs of the Coming of Christ* (Arlington: Discovery Ministries, 1998), 149.

1. Read 1 John 2:18–23.

   a. What is the implication of "you have heard" in verse 18? (How widespread was the church's understanding of the Antichrist?)

   b. What is the difference between "the Antichrist" (is coming) and "many antichrists" (have come)? (verse 18)

   c. What did "the antichrists" do that identified them to John? (verse 19)

   d. What were the antichrists teaching that was indicative of their nature? (verse 22; see also 1 John 4:3)

   e. What doctrine is essential to Christianity? (verses 22–23)

f. What will "the" Antichrist do in the future that is consistent with verses 22–23? (see 2 Thessalonians 2:4)

2. Explain what John means in 1 John 4:3 about the "spirit of the Antichrist" that is "now already in the world."

   a. How does that change your perspective when you hear a person state that Jesus Christ is not the Son of God?

   b. Who is the ultimate "spirit of the Antichrist" when it comes to lying about Christ? (John 8:44)

3. Read Psalm 2:1–12.

   a. How does this psalm paint a picture of what you have learned about the revival of rulers in the end-time who oppose God?

b. How do verses 6 and 9 parallel the events of Revelation 19:11–21?

c. What warning would the Antichrist be wise to heed? (verses 10–12)

d. What comfort will this psalm bring to those who become Christians during the Tribulation and are persecuted by the Antichrist?

4. Read Revelation 13:1–18.

a. What is represented by the imagery in verse 2 concerning the nature of the Antichrist?

b. What actions of the Antichrist ensure his doom? (verse 6; see also Matthew 12:31–32)

c. What is the purpose of the mark that this beast gives? (verse 17)

DID YOU KNOW?

When president Ronald Reagan and his wife, Nancy, left the White House, they moved to a home that had been purchased for them in Bel Air, California. The address was 666 St. Cloud Road. Upon discovering the street number of the house, the Reagans immediately filed a request with the city to have the address number changed to 668—a request which was granted. This request had less to do with biblical conviction than general superstition on the part of the former president and first lady. But it is evident of the general dislike of many for the number of "the man of sin" (2 Thessalonians 2:3) in Scripture.[3]

3. Laurie Becklund, "The Reagans: First Family Easing Into Private Life," *Los Angeles Times*, Nov. 19, 1988.

THE NEW AXIS OF EVIL

Ezekiel 38–39

In this lesson we learn the identity of the nations that war against Israel—and how Israel is saved.

OUTLINE

The Promised Land of Israel is the most embattled land in the world. And there are more battles yet to come. The largest in history will be a coalition of armies from the north that attack Israel following the Rapture of the church. Except for God's intervention, Israel would be destroyed.

I. **The Identity of the Nations**

II **The Invasion of the Nations**
   A. The Place of the Invasion
   B. The Period of the Invasion
   C. The Purpose of the Invasion
   D. The Particulars of the Invasion

III. **The Intervention of the Nations**
   A. The Arsenal of Weapons
   B. The Aftermath of War

IV. **The Illumination of God's Plan for the Nations**
   A. The Sovereignty of God's Plan
   B. The Simplicity of God's Purpose
   C. The Salvation of God's People

On January 29, 2002, president George W. Bush delivered his State of the Union address in which he referred to a modern-day "axis of evil" consisting of three countries: Iran, Iraq, and North Korea. He called them a "grave threat and a growing danger."[1] He was roundly criticized for using the word "evil" in describing other nations. Yes, it is a hard word, but in this case entirely accurate.

One of those three nations was on God's list of evil nations as well—as outlined in Ezekiel 38–39. In this lesson we will look at God's prophecy concerning the alignment of nations that will invade Israel in the end times. Israel will have signed a covenant with the Antichrist, the new leader of the revived Roman Empire, or European Union. She will be living in peace with her Arab and Muslim neighbors, believing that the historic conflict between Arabs and Jews is over. But a coalition of nations, under the leadership of Russia, will march against Israel to wipe her off the map (to use the words of Iran's current president Mahmoud Ahmadinejad).

THE IDENTITY OF THE NATIONS

The prophet Ezekiel identifies the nations involved in Ezekiel 38:1–6, 16. This invasion is usually referred to as the "prophecy of Gog and Magog" since they are the first proper names mentioned in 38:2. The challenge today is to identify the modern descendants of Gog, Magog, and the other nations Ezekiel lists.

"Gog" is mentioned 11 times in Ezekiel 38–39. Gog was not a nation but the ruler of a land called Magog. Magog is the region on a world map where the "-stan" countries exist today—the states of the former Soviet Empire: Kazakhstan, Kyrgyzstan, Uzbekistan, Turkmenistan, Tajikistan, and perhaps Afghanistan. These nations, while independent today, were once satellite states of the former Soviet Empire. So Magog is the land that was once part of the Soviet Union.

Next mentioned is "the prince of Rosh, Meshech, and Tubal" (38:2). Ezekiel 38:6 says these invading armies will be coming from "the far north," and that has to be the realm today known as Russia (not to mention the etymological connection between Rosh and Russia). The people of Rosh in Ezekiel's day lived beyond the modern Black Sea—again, the realm of modern Russia. Twenty years ago when the former Soviet Union collapsed, no one would have imagined Russia becoming an invading force. But in recent years, under the leadership of president Vladimir Putin, Russia has emerged as a world power once again. Meshech and Tubal refer to regions that are part of modern Turkey.

In verse 5 we have "Persia, Ethiopia, and Libya," the latter two existing today under their ancient names. Persia is the ancient name for the modern nation of Iran, the name-change occurring in March, 1935. Four decades later, Iran changed its name again to the Islamic Republic of Iran. Today it is a hotbed of militant, Islamic, anti-Semitic activity. It is Iran's president, Ahmadinejad, who has publicly stated that Israel should be wiped off the map of the world. Libya today is controlled by the militant Arab ruler Colonel Mu'ammar Gadhafi. Next (verse 6) is Gomer which is also known to have been in the region of Turkey, as is "the house of Togarmah."

The tiny nation of Israel is surrounded by these much larger nations. Any of them alone would constitute a major threat—but combined? There would be little hope on a purely human basis for Israel surviving an attack from such a coalition. Israel, against overwhelming odds, won wars against enemies who attacked in 1967 (the Six-Days War) and in 1973 (the Yom Kippur War)—but the coalition described in Ezekiel 38 would be like nothing she has faced before (see Figure 6).

THE INVASION OF THE NATIONS

We can determine the place, period, and purpose of the invasion of these nations from Ezekiel's prophecy.

The Place of the Invasion

Verse 8 refers to those "brought back from the sword and . . . brought out of the nations." That obviously refers to Israel who "dwell[s] safely" in her land (see also 38:11, 12, 14, 16 that repeat these same identifiers and more). Ezekiel saw Israel gathered from the nations and dwelling in peace in her own land. That's where the invasion takes place.

The Period of the Invasion

It's going to happen "after many days" (38:8), "in the latter days" (38:16), when Israel is back in the land dwelling safely (38:14). Has there ever been a time when Israel has lived "safely" in her own land? They were attacked the first week after being recognized as a nation in 1948 and have been attacked ever since. She has never dwelt in peace and safety in the modern era.

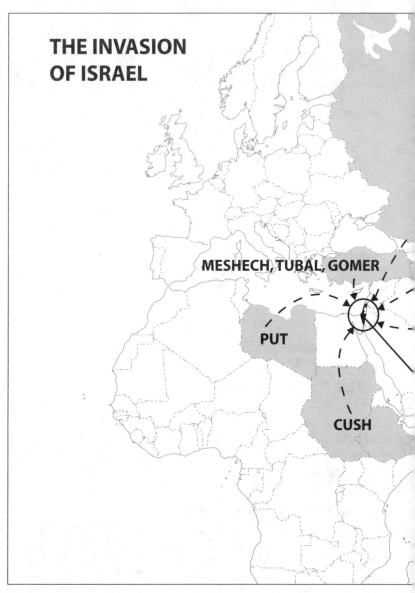

THE INVASION OF ISRAEL

MESHECH, TUBAL, GOMER

PUT

CUSH

Figure 6

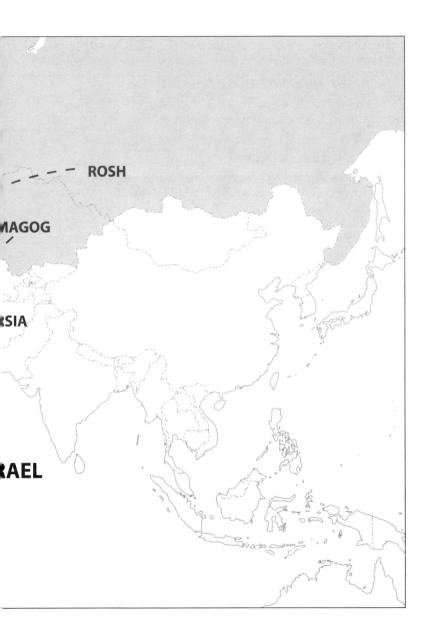

ROSH

MAGOG

RSIA

RAEL

But that day will come following the Rapture of the church. The European Union (revived Roman Empire) will send their ruler to Israel who will make a peace treaty with Israel—a covenant to protect Israel against her enemies (Daniel 9:27). It will be when Israel relaxes, believing she is protected, that the invasion will come.

The Purpose of the Invasion

There will be three purposes of the invasion—the same reasons nations have attacked throughout history: land, wealth, and people.

1. To Seize Israel's Land

Verse 38:12 refers to "the waste places that are again inhabited." There are many reasons Israel's land would be desired, not the least of which to turn it over to the Palestinians who have contested the land with Israel for decades. But the wealth Israel has developed in terms of natural resources, agriculture, and potentially oil would be invaluable.

2. To Steal Israel's Wealth

The invaders will come "to take plunder and to take booty." They will stretch out their hands "against a people . . . who have acquired livestock and goods" (38:12). They will come to take "silver and gold" and "great plunder" (38:13). Israel today is a wealthy land; the number of millionaires is far out of proportion to her population of seven million. The Jewish people have a God-given gift for accumulating wealth, and these invading nations will come to grab it.

3. To Slaughter Israel's People

The common denominator among the modern descendants of the nations Ezekiel mentions is their resistance to, if not hatred for, Israel. And Ezekiel says these nations will "stretch out [their] hand" (38:12) against Israel and "come up against . . . Israel like a cloud, to cover the land" (38:16). Their goal will be just as it was in the Nazi Holocaust—genocide against the Jewish race.

The Particulars of the Invasion

There is only one particular that needs to be discussed from Israel's perspective: God himself. Without God, Israel would be destroyed completely, but when God arrives on the scene, she will be saved. Here is the formula: Desperation + God = Hope. It doesn't matter what the circumstance is; when God arrives, there is hope.

The Intervention of the Nations

Israel has pulled off military miracles in her history, and she will need another one when Russia and the other nations come against her. And that is what she will get when God arrives on the scene: "'And it will come to pass at the same time, when Gog comes against the land of Israel,' says the Lord God, 'that My fury will show in My face. For in My jealousy and in the fire of My wrath I have spoken'" (38:18–19a).

The Arsenal of Weapons

God doesn't bring guns and swords to the battle but four weapons even more powerful.

1. By the Convulsions of the Earth

Verses 38:19–20 describe "a great earthquake in the land of Israel." Some people might not understand the severity of this event, but those of us who live in California do. Scientists talk about "the big one" referring to a giant earthquake likely to hit California some day. But this one in Israel is going to be *the* "big one."

2. By the Confusion of the Troops

Convulsions in the earth will result in confusion among the armies: "I will call for a sword against Gog throughout all My mountains," says the Lord God. "Every man's sword will be against his brother" (38:21).

All these nations with their different languages and cultures will find themselves at war with one another when God begins to throw down the mountains and the "steep places" around them (38:20). Something similar happened in Judges 7–8 to the 135,000 Midianites gathered against Israel.

3. By the Contagion of Disease

"Pestilence" will accompany the carnage ("bloodshed") that takes place when God intervenes with convulsions in the earth and confusion among the armies (38:22a).

4. By the Calamities from the Sky

The end result will be like Sodom and Gomorrah (Genesis 19:24) all over again: "flooding rain, great hailstones, fire, and brimstone" (38:22b). Consider these words from *The Pulpit Commentary:* "Every force of nature is a servant of the living God. And in a moment, He can make the forces of nature into His soldiers, armed to the teeth. Men are slowly discovering that God's forces stored in nature are mightier than the brawn of the human arm."[2]

Before this war ever gets started, God routs the armies, destroys their purposes, and saves Israel from destruction yet again.

The Aftermath of War

Three events will happen in the aftermath of this great carnage: a feast, a funeral, and a fire.

1. A Feast

Verse 39:4 talks about a feast in which the armies of the north are invited—and they are the main course! The "birds of prey of every sort" and the "beasts of the field" devour the fallen armies. God tells Ezekiel to call the birds and beasts to feast on the bodies of the fallen soldiers (39:17–20).

2. A Funeral

The remains from the feast will still need to be buried: "For seven months the house of Israel will be burying them, in order to cleanse the land" (39:12). A funeral that lasts seven months gives some idea of the extent of the carnage after God intervenes. A dead body creates ceremonial as well as hygienic uncleanness in the laws of Israel, so burial will be a necessity.

3. A Fire

In verses 39:9–10, Ezekiel used the language of his day to describe the time it will take to clean up and dispose of the remains of war: weapons, equipment, and the like. Ezekiel says they will be burned—whether that is true (perhaps melted down?) remains to be seen. Again, Ezekiel was describing wooden bows and arrows, chariots, and other weapons of his day. Regardless of how it happens, there will be a massive reclamation project where the weapons of war are recycled.

THE ILLUMINATION OF GOD'S PLAN FOR THE NATIONS

Thankfully, before any of this comes to pass, you and I (that is, all true believers in Christ) will have been removed from earth at the Rapture. This conflagration in Israel takes place sometime after that during the first half of the Tribulation. We will watch the War of Gog and Magog from the portals of heaven.

Regardless of Christians being absent, we can still learn much from what unfolds in the future.

The Sovereignty of God's Plan

God orchestrates everything in His creation. It is He who brings about the destruction of the enemies of His chosen people.

In 38:4 God says, "I will turn you around, put hooks into your jaws, and lead you out." "Hooks into your jaws" is a fisherman's term—when a hook is set in a fish, the fisherman can take him wherever he wants. So God says to Russia that He will lead them where He wants them to go—in this case, to Israel where they will be destroyed. He uses the active verb "bring" in verses 38:16 and 39:2 to describe His leadership in this situation. God's plan is sovereign; the nations of the world do His bidding.

God never puts evil into anyone's heart. But when nations set out to do evil, God orchestrates their just desserts. The principle of reaping what we sow (Galatians 6:7) is always at work according to God's sovereign purposes in the world. God does not sit in heaven watching expectantly to see where the nations and armies of the world move. Instead, He is the one moving them by His sovereign will.

The Simplicity of God's Purpose

God's glory in the earth is always His purpose and this battle is no exception: "I will bring you against My land, so that the nations may know Me, when I am hallowed in you, O God, before their eyes" (38:16). This theme is repeated again and again in these two chapters of Ezekiel: 38:23; 39:6–7. Verses 39:21–22 summarize God's purpose eloquently: "I will set My glory among the nations; all the nations shall see My judgment which I have executed, and My hand which I have laid on them. So the house of Israel shall know that I am the Lord their God from that day forward."

We live in a day when God's name and His glory are roundly criticized and caricatured around the world—and especially here in the United States. But God is not oblivious to the defaming of His name. His glory and sovereign power will ultimately be revealed in the works of man's hands as he brings them to frustration and His purposes to fruition. The world will one day witness the vindication of who He is and what He is doing to accomplish His plans. The communication systems in place in that day will broadcast the destruction of these armies around the world for all the world to see.

The Salvation of God's People

God has a purpose for Israel in all this as well: the restoration of His chosen people to himself. Ezekiel 39:27–29 says, "'When I have brought them back from the peoples and gathered them out of their enemies' lands, and I am hallowed in them in the sight of many nations, then they shall know that I am the Lord their God, who sent them into captivity among the nations, but also brought them back to their land, and left none of them captive any longer. And I will not hide My face from them anymore; for I shall have poured out My Spirit on the house of Israel,' says the Lord God."

Romans 11 teaches us that Israel would be set aside for a time while the Gospel was taken to the Gentile nations of the world, and that has happened. But now they are being drawn back to their Promised Land, and many Jews have come to believe in Jesus (Yeshua) as their true Messiah. This turning will culminate in the last part of the Tribulation when Jesus returns and Israel "shall look on Him whom they pierced" (Zechariah 12:10; John 19:37).

Are you ready to meet Him when He comes for His church? Do not delay—make your decision for Christ today.

Notes:

1. http://www.whitehouse.gov/news/release/2002/01/print/20020129–11.html.
2. H.D.M. Spence and Joseph Excell, eds. *The Pulpit Commentary, Vol. 28* (London and NY: Funk and Wagnalls, 1880–93), 298.

APPLICATION

1. Read Jeremiah 31:31–37.

   a. What is God going to do one day, and how will it be different from the covenant God made with Israel's forefathers? (31–33; see Exodus 34:12)

   b. Why will there be no need for "evangelism" in that day? (34)

   c. What will be the basis of this covenant? (34b)

   d. What natural signs has God established to ensure the fulfillment of this covenant promise? (35–37)

   e. If we ever witness a disruption in the solar system or reach its outer limits, what will you know is true about the nation of Israel?

2. From Ezekiel 37, answer the following questions:

   a. In order for God to fulfill His promised covenant to Israel (Jeremiah 31:31–37), what would have to happen to Israel? (Who do the bones in 1–10 represent? See 11.)

   b. What is the purpose of the image of the valley of dry bones? (12, 21)

   c. What lesson is to be taught to the nation when she is once again established in the land? (13–14)

   d. How does 23 confirm, in a practical way, the promises of Jeremiah 31:34b?

e. Who will rule over Israel in that day, and how do we know this refers to Jesus Christ? (Isaiah 11:1–3; Matthew 1:1; 3:16–17; 12:23; Ezekiel 34:23–24)

g. Describe the condition under which Israel will live under "David" as king. (24–28)

3. Having studied Ezekiel 38–39 in this lesson, how do those chapters connect with Ezekiel 37? What needed to happen to Israel's enemies for the promises of God to Israel to be fulfilled?

4. From Romans 11:1–36, answer the following:

a. What will ultimately happen to Israel? (26–27)

b. Given the view of God's sovereign plan, why is 33–36 the proper response?

DID YOU KNOW?

To get an idea of how one-sided a war between Russia/Iran and Israel would be, compare these vital statistics (numbers approximate and rounded):

	Russia/Iran Combined	Israel
Size	7.2 million square miles	8,500 square miles
Gross Domestic Product (2007)	$2.3 trillion	$233 billion
Active Duty Military	1.5 million troops	168,000 troops
Nuclear Weapons?	Russia: Yes (world's largest supply) Iran: Developing	Yes

ARMING FOR ARMAGEDDON

Revelation 16:13–16; Daniel 11:36–45

*In this lesson we learn about earth's final war—
and how it ends.*

OUTLINE

The word "Armageddon" is used in modern cultures to describe doomsday-type events—or even a "meeting with the boss." Many people don't know it is the biblical name for earth's final great battle—when Israel is saved from annihilation and the rebellious nations of earth are defeated.

I. **The Preparation for the Battle of Armageddon**

II. **The Place of the Battle of Armageddon**

III. **The Purpose of the Battle of Armageddon**
 A. To Finish His Judgment upon Israel
 B. To Finalize His Judgment upon the Nations That Have Persecuted Israel
 C. To Formally Judge All the Nations That Have Rejected Him

IV. **The Perspective of the Battle of Armageddon**

V. **The Participants in the Battle of Armageddon**
 A. The Deal Between Israel and Antichrist
 B. The Demand that Everyone Worship the Antichrist
 C. The Decision to Fight Against the Antichrist
 D. The Disturbing News from the East
 E. The Descending Lord from the Heavens

America is no stranger to war. Since the beginning of our nation, we have experienced a major war about every twenty-five years beginning with the Revolutionary War, the War of 1812, the Civil War, The Spanish-American War, World Wars I and II, the Korean War, the Vietnam War, the Persian Gulf War, and the wars in Afghanistan and Iraq. Hardly any generation has been able to live their whole life without sending their young to war.

The Bible says there is going to be a final war one day on this earth. That war, called Armageddon, will signal the coming down of the curtain on modern civilization. And preparation for that war is under way in our world at this very moment. The only thing blocking the players in that war from moving onto the stage of battle is the Rapture—the transfer of the church of Jesus Christ to heaven. Following that event, the final war—the Battle of Armageddon—will take place.

THE PREPARATION FOR THE BATTLE OF ARMAGEDDON

The Battle of Armageddon begins in heaven and descends to earth with the casting out of Satan (Revelation 12:9–13). Satan is the "prince of the power of the air" (Ephesians 2:2)—his dominion is the heavenly region surrounding planet earth. But in the middle of the seven-year Tribulation, he will be cast out of that domain to earth where he will begin to persecute "the woman who gave birth to the male Child" (Revelation 12:13). The "woman" is not Mary, Jesus' mother, but Israel—the one through whom Jesus Christ came into this world. Satan's goal will be to destroy Israel before the return of Christ to establish His kingdom on earth.

Satan will have two human helpers: the beast and the false prophet (Revelation 16:13). These three form an unholy trinity of persecution against God's chosen people during the Tribulation. And it is that reign of terror against Israel that will lead the world to the Battle of Armageddon.

THE PLACE OF THE BATTLE OF ARMAGEDDON

Revelation 16:16 identifies Armageddon as a place in the Holy Land. "Armageddon" is a Hebrew word made up of two smaller words: "har" (mountain) and "Megiddo" (slaughter). So Armageddon is "mountain of slaughter." I once stood on a hill overlooking the vast Plain of Megiddo in northern Israel—twenty miles southeast of Haifa and fifty miles north of Israel. In 1799 the French conqueror Napoleon stood at Megiddo and declared, "All the armies of the world could maneuver their forces on this vast plain. There is no place in the whole world more suited for war than this. It is the most natural battleground on the whole earth."[1]

The battle of Armageddon will not be fought only at Megiddo— it will spill over into all of Israel and even other parts of the world. Joel says there will be fighting in "the Valley of Jehoshaphat" which is east of Jerusalem (Joel 3:2). Isaiah says the sword will fall on Edom which was south of the Dead Sea (Isaiah 34:5). And Zechariah refers to Jerusalem as being part of the stage of battle (Zechariah 12:2).

Revelation 14:20 says blood will flow "up to the horses' bridles, for one thousand six hundred furlongs." That distance in furlongs is about 200 miles—exactly the distance from one end of Israel to the other. The "horses' bridles" reference is an ancient one probably referring to quantity. In other words, a great deal of blood is going to be spilled in the Battle of Armageddon.

THE PURPOSE OF THE BATTLE OF ARMAGEDDON

Why would God allow such a blood-bath to take place on earth? There are three biblical reasons.

To Finish God's Judgment upon Israel

For all the sympathy it is easy to feel toward Israel during this period when she is being attacked by others, we have to remember that she is still living in rebellion toward God. Even the reestablishment of the nation in 1948 was more a Zionist cultural, political movement than a spiritual one. Israel to this day has not embraced her Messiah, and judgment will fall upon her for that reason. It is that judgment that will cause many Jews during the Tribulation to turn to God and accept the Messiah they rejected (Zechariah 12:10).

To Finalize His Judgment upon the Nations That Have Persecuted Israel

As God allows the nations of the world to inflict judgment upon Israel, He will be inflicting judgment on them: "I will also gather all nations, and bring them down to the Valley of Jehoshaphat; and I will enter into judgment with them there" (Joel 3:2).

In the first lesson in this study guide, we noted God's promise to "curse those who curse [Abraham and his descendants]" (Genesis 12:3). And that is why these nations of the world will be judged during the wars that make up Armageddon.

To Formally Judge All the Nations That Have Rejected Him

Revelation 19:15 says that God will "tread the winepress of the fierceness of the wrath of Almighty God." Not only will the nations be judged because they have attacked Israel but also because they have rejected God and His Son, the Lord Jesus Christ. Psalm 2 pictures the Lord in heaven laughing at the "kings of the earth" who "take counsel together" against God and His Anointed. But they will be judged for their rejection of Him.

THE PERSPECTIVE OF THE BATTLE OF ARMAGEDDON

Let's reset the stage for this end-time conflagration: The church of Jesus Christ is Raptured to heaven which marks the beginning of the seven-year Tribulation period. The ruler of the European nations, the Antichrist, makes a peace treaty with Israel ensuring her safety from the surrounding Arab nations—a time when Israel is living in "unwalled villages" (Ezekiel 38:11). During this time the coalition of nations from "the north" (Russia, Iran, and others) attack Israel but is stopped and defeated by God: the Battle of Gog and Magog. This is not the Battle of Armageddon—these two battles need to be kept separate:

Gog and Magog	Armageddon
• Russia, Iran, and at least five other nations	• All the nations of the world
• Invaders come from the north	• Invaders come from all directions
• Purpose is to take Israel's wealth and land	• Purpose is to annihilate the Jews and fight against Christ and His armies as they return to earth
• Russia will be the leader	• The Antichrist will be the leader
• Invaders are defeated by earthquake and disease	• Invaders are defeated by Christ
• Those killed limited to land of Israel	• Armies killed all over the earth
• The dead will be buried	• Dead will be consumed by birds
• Not the final battle on earth	• The final war before the Millennium begins [2]

THE PARTICIPANTS IN THE BATTLE OF ARMAGEDDON

There are five major stages in the Battle of Armageddon—beginning with the treaty between Israel and the Antichrist.

The Deal Between Israel and the Antichrist

Daniel 9:27 is the verse that tells us about the "covenant" (treaty) the Antichrist makes with Israel—a seven-year peace-protection pledge. From his position of power in the revived Roman Empire (Europe)—and his apparent resurrection from an assassination—he begins to accumulate power and "speak blasphemies against the God of gods" (Daniel 11:36). The "god" of his own strength and power is the only god he worships (Daniel 11:37–39).

With this power he convinces Israel to enter into a treaty that will protect Israel from the growing storm of threats against her in the world—specifically from her Arab neighbors.

The Demand that Everyone Worship the Antichrist

If you think the world is looking for answers today to problems like global climate change, food shortages, gas prices, and warring nations, it is only going to be worse in the future. Life in the future is not going to get easier, it's going to get harder. When the Antichrist rises to the stage of power, people will be eager to submit to him. His seeming supernatural abilities will cause people to see him as the savior of mankind.

But after signing the peace treaty with Israel, he makes a mistake: he demands that people worship him under threat of death (Revelation 13:15). Some of the earth's peoples rebel at this extension of the Antichrist's power, which sets the stage for the next movement.

The Decision to Fight Against the Antichrist

Daniel 11:40 says that the "king of the South" and "the king of the North" will attack the Antichrist. If you consider that many nations of the world have strong religious heritages—especially Muslim nations—it's not difficult to see how some would resist, even refuse, the idea of worshipping the Antichrist as a god. So they decide to move against him and remove him from power.

Daniel's prophecy describes a great army from Africa, including not only Egypt, but other countries of the continent. The army, probably numbering in the millions, will attack the Middle East from the south. And at the same time, Russia and other armies from the north will mobilize another powerful military force. Even though Russia may have lost a lot of its people and military four years earlier in the Battle of Gog and Magog, they will apparently have recovered enough to begin to recoup their losses and get involved in this battle again. And so what happens at the beginning is, the Antichrist is all puffed up with his power demanding the worship of the world and here are the armies of the North and the South coming and saying, "We're going to take this guy out. We'll not have him do this to us." [3]

The Disturbing News from the East

As the Antichrist is resisting the armies from the south and the north, "news from the east and the north shall trouble him; therefore he shall go out with great fury to destroy and annihilate many" (Daniel 11:44). Suddenly the Antichrist is being attacked from all different directions. Revelation 16:12 pictures a great army coming from the east over a dried-up River Euphrates. The number of that army coming from the East is 200 million (Revelation 9:16). Many Bible students stumble at the thought of a 200-million-man army. But it would not be difficult, given the population of China alone, for a coalition of countries from the east (Asia) to field an army of 200 million soldiers.

So the Antichrist is facing armies coming at him from all directions. But there is a supernatural component to this: "For they are the spirits of demons, performing signs, which go out to the kings of the earth of the whole world, to gather them to the battle of that great day of God Almighty" (Revelation 16:14).

The Descending Lord from the Heavens

These armies are moving toward Israel under the inspiration of Satan himself. Satan's goal, of course, is to gather all the armies of the world to attack Israel and destroy her for good. The problem is that, while everyone has been checking north, south, east and west, they have forgotten to check "up." If they had, they would have seen the Lord Jesus Christ himself descending with His armies from heaven:

Now I saw heaven opened, and behold, a white horse. And He who sat on him was called Faithful and True, and in righteousness He judges and makes war. His eyes were like a flame of fire, and on His head were many crowns. He had a name written that no one knew except himself. He was clothed with a robe dipped in blood, and His name is called The Word of God. And the armies in heaven, clothed in fine linen, white and clean, followed Him on white horses. Now out of His mouth goes a sharp sword, that with it He should strike the nations. And He himself will rule them with a rod of iron. He himself treads the winepress of the fierceness and wrath of Almighty God. And He has on His robe and on His thigh a name written: KING OF KINGS AND LORD OF LORDS (Revelation 19:11–16).

Israel suddenly gets reinforcements from the sky—reinforcements no one had anticipated. And it changes the entire battle scene. The armies that return with Jesus Christ are made up of saints—all true believers who were Raptured off the earth prior to the Tribulation—and angels. If you are a Christian, you will be part of this army that descends from heaven with Christ.

1. Descending with All His Saints

Several verses in Scripture refer to the appearance of God with His saints at the end of time: Zechariah 14:5; 1 Thessalonians 3:13; 2 Thessalonians 1:10; Jude 1:14. Think of the number of saints this represents—all the faithful from the beginning of time who were resurrected at the Rapture—including those who were alive on earth at the Rapture! That's how they got to heaven.

It is a finite number, but one that is too large to consider estimating. At the least, it is a number that will make the gathered armies of earth look puny in scope. The column of saints coming behind Christ on His white horse (Revelation 19:11) will be the most awe-inspiring sight in all of human history and will no doubt strike fear in the hearts of all on earth.

2. Descending with All His Angels

Along with the saints from the ages will come the heavenly hosts—the angels of heaven: "When the Son of Man comes in His glory, and all the holy angels with Him, then He will sit on the throne of His glory" (Matthew 25:31; see also 2 Thessalonians 1:7).

Christians are going to fight side-by-side with angels! But wait—there is no record in Scripture of us lifting a single finger in the fight. Rather, it is the "sharp sword" going "out of [Christ's] mouth" with which He "strike[s] the nations" (Revelation 19:15). That "sharp sword" is not a literal sword. Because it comes out of His mouth it is a metaphor for the words of judgment He will speak, words that will signal the end of the rebellious armies of earth. He will speak and it will be over.

So what is our purpose on that day? It is the same as we have seen in other settings where God intervenes: so that His glory might be revealed to us. Second Thessalonians 1:10 says that on that day He will be "glorified in His saints and . . . admired among all those who believe." All the saints of the ages—that great "cloud of witnesses" (Hebrews 12:1)—will witness Christ in all His glory pronounce judgment on those who oppose God and His people, the Jews.

In a day when Israel has no earthly allies by her side, the only true ally she has ever had, her own Messiah, saves her from destruction. If you want to see the greatest battle in history ended with a word, make sure you are among the armies of heaven who return with Christ and witness His judgment.

Notes:

1. J. Vernon McGee, *Through the Bible, Vol. 3* (Nashville: Thomas Nelson, 1982), 513.
2. Adapted from Carl G. Johnson, *Prophecy Made Plain for Times Like This* (Chicago: Moody Press, 1972), 169–170.
3. John Walvoord with Mark Hitchcock, *Armageddon, Oil and Terror* (Carol Stream: Tyndale House, 2007), 174.

1. From Revelation 16, describe the events that take place prior to, and at, Armageddon.

   a. By whose authority are the events leading to Armageddon ordered? (verse 1)

   b. What do the seven bowls in verse 1 represent?

   c. What did the first angel pour out on those worshipping the Antichrist? (verse 2)

   d. What happened to the oceans as a result of the second angel's bowl? (verse 3)

   e. What ironic interpretation did the third angel give to the effects of the third bowl judgment? (verses 4–6)

   f. Who does the voice of the "altar" represent in verse 7? (Revelation 6:9. Why would this group agree with the angel's statement in verses 5–6)

   g. What was the content of the fourth bowl judgment? (verse 8)

   h. What was the content of the fifth angel's bowl? (verse 10)

i. What did the sixth angel's bowl accomplish? (verse 12)

j. How do we know that the Antichrist and his False Prophet will be demonically possessed? (verses 13–14)

k. What happens when the seventh angel pours out his bowl? (verses 17–21)

l. Compare the words coming from the temple (verse 17) with the words spoken in John 19:30? How are they two different aspects of the same conclusion?

2. From what you have learned so far in this study guide, what is the only way to avoid the calamitous events described in Revelation 16?

DID YOU KNOW?

We speak of the "battle" of Armageddon as if it was a one-time event—a single battle. In reality, it is more of a war or a campaign. The Greek word translated "battle" in the book of Revelation and other places in the New Testament occurs a total of eighteen times and is translated "wars" or "war" as often as battle. A war or military campaign is made up of many battles and such will be the Battle of Armageddon. It will involve many battles fought throughout the land of Israel over a three-and-one-half year period of time. *The* Battle of Armageddon usually refers to the culminating event in which Christ defeats the gathered foes of God—the last battle in the lengthy war.

THE RETURN OF THE KING

Revelation 19:11–21

*In this lesson we study the details of
Christ's victory in earth's greatest battle.*

OUTLINE

Planet earth's most amazing day is yet to come: The largest massing of armies in world history will turn their faces skyward to see Jesus Christ descending from the clouds with His own armies. By the word of His mouth, He will pronounce judgment upon all who rebel against God.

I. The Anticipation of Christ

II. The Advent of Christ
   A. The Designation of Christ
   B. The Description of Christ

III. The Armies of Christ

IV. The Authority of Christ

V. The Avenging of Christ
   A. The Fowls of Heaven
   B. The Foes of Heaven

VI. The Application of Christ's Second Coming
   A. We Should Refrain from Judging Others
   B. We Should Remember the Lord's Table
   C. We Can Relate to One Another in Love
   D. We Can Recommit Ourselves to Ministry
   E. We Must Refuse to Neglect the Church
   F. We Must Reach the Lost for Jesus Christ

The first and second comings of Christ are both important—but they are very different. Note the following comparisons:

Christ's First Coming	Christ's Second Coming
• Clothed in swaddling clothes	• Clothed in a robe dipped in blood
• Surrounded by cattle and common people	• Surrounded by armies of saints and angels
• The door of the inn was closed to Him	• The door of heaven is opened for Him
• His voice was the cry of a baby	• His voice is like the sound of many waters
• The Lamb of God for salvation	• The Lion of the Tribe of Judah for judgment

In this final lesson on the prophetic future of planet earth, we examine the climax of all prophetic Scriptures: the return of Jesus Christ to earth to reign as King of Kings and Lord of Lords.

THE ANTICIPATION OF CHRIST

Next to faith, the Second Coming of Christ is the most dominant subject in the New Testament. For every one time the first advent of Christ is mentioned, the Second Coming is mentioned eight times. Jesus himself is recorded as mentioning His Second Coming twenty-one times. There are 333 prophecies about Christ in the Bible, but only 109 were fulfilled at His first coming leaving 224 to be fulfilled at the Second Coming.

Christ's Second Coming is mentioned throughout the Bible. Zechariah the prophet mentions it (Zechariah 14:4), angels mention it (Acts 1:11), Jesus declared He would return (Matthew 24:17, 29), the apostle John confirmed it (Revelation 1:7)—just to mention a few.

Never let anyone tell you that the Second Coming of Christ is immaterial to the message of the Bible. It is a central doctrine and must be taught as part of the whole counsel of God.

THE ADVENT OF CHRIST

Revelation 19 is the central prophetic passage in Scripture on the actual return of Jesus Christ to earth. When He returns it will be to the same place from which He ascended: the Mount of Olives in Jerusalem (Acts 1:10–12).

The Designation of Christ

There are three different names given to Christ in Revelation 19: "Faithful and True" (verse 11), "The Word of God" (verse 13), and "King of Kings and Lord of Lords" (verse 16). Those names represent Him and His ministry: His unchanging nature from eternity past (Hebrews 13:8), His incarnation as the living Word (John 1:14), and His future role as ruler of God's kingdom (Luke 1:32).

The Description of Christ

Revelation 19:12–13 gives a magnificent description of Christ: eyes like flaming fire and a head on which were many crowns, clothed in a robe dipped in blood. Eyes of fire mean there will be no posturing or pretending in His presence. His eyes will burn away all pretense and see men's hearts as they really are. The multiple crowns speak of His ultimate kingship over all the so-called kings of the earth, making Him worthy for every knee to bow before Him (Philippians 2:10). The robe dipped in blood reminds us that He is the "Lamb who was slain before the foundation of the world" (Revelation 13:8).

I believe throughout eternity the representation of the Lord Jesus Christ we will see is as the Lamb of God. We will see His nail-scarred palms and His spear-wounded side and be reminded for all eternity that He is the only reason we are there. We will have the same response that the apostle John had when he said, "Behold! The Lamb of God who takes away the sin of the world!" (John 1:29)

THE ARMIES OF CHRIST

In the previous lesson we noted that the armies who return with Christ are all the saints of the ages—having been in heaven since the Rapture, seven years prior—and the angels. In verse 14 we learn how we will appear: "clothed in fine linen, white and clean, [following] Him on white horses." Soldiers normally don't wear white into battle, but in this case it's okay because we are not actually going to enter into combat. It is the word of His judgment (the "sharp sword" going out of His mouth) that carries the day. Jude 14–15 gives the most detailed explanation of the reasons for this judgment: "to convict all who are ungodly among them of their ungodly deeds . . . and of all the harsh things which ungodly sinners have spoken against Him."

When Christ returns, it is primarily for judgment. Remember that most of the people on the earth at this time have rejected the 144,000 evangelists (Revelation 14:1) and two witnesses (Revelation 11:3–14) that God sends during the Tribulation. In other words, they are deserving of judgment. God never sends judgment without first having sent a warning or an opportunity to believe. But a time will come when judgment is no longer delayed.

THE AUTHORITY OF CHRIST

When Christ returns, the parts of Isaiah 9:6–7 that were not fulfilled in His first coming will be fulfilled: He will assume His place on the throne of His forefather David and "of the increase of His government and peace there will be no end." There was never a time in His first coming that "the government [was] upon His shoulder." The Old Testament prophets saw truth in their prophetic vision—in this case, the complete picture of God's Messiah—but they did not always see the timing. They did not see the gap of time between His first and second coming.

When He returns, He will rule with the authority given to the throne of David in Israel. He will "strike the nations" and "rule them with a rod of iron" (verse 15). And there will be no end to His authority, government, and the resulting peace.

THE AVENGING OF CHRIST

The Battle of Armageddon is where justice is meted out upon the ungodly on this earth (verses 17–21).

The Fowls of Heaven

An angel in heaven calls to "all the birds that fly in the midst of heaven" for them to "gather together for the supper of the great God"—meaning for them to consume the flesh of the armies killed in the last battle when Christ returns (verses 17–18). These are essentially vultures that come to pick over the bones of the dead after the massive destruction of humanity.

This supper to which the vultures are called is the second supper described in Revelation 19, the first being the Marriage Supper of the Lamb (verse 9)—the celebration of the union between Christ and His church in heaven. I strongly suggest making reservations now for the Marriage Supper of the Lamb rather than "the supper of the great God."

The Foes of Heaven

Even though the Antichrist's doom is sealed, he still gathers the armies of earth to fight against the returning Christ.

1. The Futility of Fighting Against God

Verse 19 presents something almost unbelievable: "And I saw the beast, the kings of the earth, and their armies, gathered together to make war against Him who sat on the horse and against His army." The Antichrist is obviously a very intelligent human being, but this is not a smart move on his part: going up against the Son of God in battle. This is the ultimate act of rebellion of Satan, the one inspiring the Antichrist—a last-ditch effort to inspire humanity to shake its collective fist in the face of God. This attempt, like all others, will be futile.

2. The Fatality of the Beast and the False Prophet

The Beast and the False Prophet were captured and "were cast alive into the lake of fire burning with brimstone" (verse 20). The "lake of fire" is, of course, eternal hell. Satan, the one who inspired them, will end up there as well, but a thousand years later (Revelation 20:7–10). During the Millennium Satan is confined but set free near the end. He foments a rebellion against Christ but is judged and confined to the lake of fire along with the Beast and the False Prophet where they will be "tormented day and night forever and ever" (Revelation 20:10).

It's a sad fact that nobody talks about hell anymore—especially preachers. But there's more in the Bible about hell than about heaven. It will be a shame someday for people to be facing an eternity in hell because the reality of that place was never mentioned in the churches they attended for years. Preachers shouldn't preach on hell every Sunday, but they definitely should preach on it when and where it occurs in the biblical text. To avoid it is to deny people the truth. The fact that Satan, the Antichrist, and the False Prophet all spend eternity there makes it an unsavory place for people to go. We ought to be honest about the reality of hell so at least people know what their future holds if they choose to reject Jesus Christ.

3. The Finality of Christ's Victory over Rebellion

With Satan bound for a thousand years, Christ will rule an earthly kingdom of peace, righteousness, and justice. He will sit on the throne and oversee the turning of implements of war into implements of agriculture and peace (Isaiah 2:4; Micah 4:3). There will be no war during the Millennium and only a short rebellion at the end when Satan is loosed from his chains in preparation for his judgment. The human race will experience for the first time what it means to live under the rule and reign of God himself.

THE APPLICATION OF CHRIST'S SECOND COMING

We have covered a lot of prophetic ground in this study guide on what is going on in the world—and will be going on in the future. I have six observations on how we should live in light of the coming end-time events.

We Should Refrain from Judging Others

In 1 Corinthians 4:5 the apostle Paul wrote, "Therefore judge nothing before the time, until the Lord comes, who will both bring to light the hidden things of darkness and reveal the counsels of the hearts. Then each one's praise will come from God."

In other words, when Christ returns He will set all the accounts right; He will judge what needs to be judged—for believers before the Millennium (1 Corinthians 3:11–15) and unbelievers at the end of the Millennium (Revelation 20:11–15). But don't misunderstand this point: "Don't judge" doesn't mean we don't call "sin" sin. It doesn't mean we don't identify evil and wickedness and immorality where we see it and take a stand against it. It means we should not jump to conclusions and condemn people when we ourselves might be guilty of the same things (Matthew 7:3–5).

We Should Remember the Lord's Table

Second, we should be faithful in "[proclaiming] the Lord's death until He comes" (1 Corinthians 11:26) by participation in the Lord's Table. When we gather as a corporate body for Communion, we look back at the death of Christ and remind ourselves of why He died. But we do that knowing it is a temporary remembrance: We do it "until He comes." So the Lord's Table keeps us mindful of Christ's death and His Second Coming at the same time.

We Can Relate to One Another in Love

First Thessalonians 3:12–13 says we should "increase and abound in love to one another and to all" so that our hearts might be "blameless . . . at the coming of our Lord Jesus Christ with all His saints."

If you recall from previous lessons, all the saints of God will be united together in the army of Christ when we return with Him at the end of the Tribulation period when He executes judgment upon the ungodly nations of the earth. Since we are going to be united then, shouldn't we live united today? That is, shouldn't we be exercising love toward one another ("and to all") in all we do now? Since we are going to spend eternity together, it behooves us to begin to live that way in our earthly relationships. There is no convincing argument for why we shouldn't.

We Can Recommit Ourselves to Ministry

This next one is primarily an exhortation to preachers like myself: "I charge you . . . Preach the word! Be ready in season and out of season. Convince, rebuke, exhort, with all longsuffering and teaching" (2 Timothy 4:1). Preachers of the Word are to be faithful, saying exactly what God says—especially as the time nears for the return of Christ. And that applies to any who minister the Word in Christ's stead until He returns: Bible study leaders, Sunday school teachers, personal counselors, campus ministry discipleship leaders, and Bible teachers in Christian schools. As the time draws near for Christ's return, peoples' opportunities to respond to the Gospel or obey the Word of God become fewer. We must speak the truth—in love, yes (Ephesians 4:15)—but always the truth.

We Must Refuse to Neglect the Church

This exhortation is for every Christian, not just those who preach or teach the Word: "Not forsaking the assembling of ourselves together, as is the manner of some, but exhorting one another, and so much the more as you see the Day approaching" (Hebrews 10:25).

"The Day" is the day of Christ's coming for His church. And as things begin to cycle downward in the last days it will take being an active part of the body of Christ to "stir up love and good works" (verse 24) as things get more and more dark. Church attendance is not just for contributing money and singing worship songs. It is to be encouraged by the Word and the Spirit and by one another! It's not easy to maintain a faithful Christian walk in today's world, and the possibility is good that it is going to get more difficult in the future.

In light of that reality, it is amazing that church attendance is falling. Churches that used to meet together on Sunday morning and evening and Wednesday night now only meet on Sunday morning. And many Christians think nothing of skipping a

Sunday morning service for the slightest of reasons. Don't be one of those. Be found in the midst of a corporate body of believers as often as possible to give and receive encouragement.

We Must Reach the Lost for Jesus Christ

Finally, we must take to heart the words of Jude: "And on some have compassion, making a distinction; but others save with fear, pulling them out of the fire" (verses 22–23).

The end times are nearer today than they were yesterday. That means we have less time than before to extend the saving Gospel of Christ to those who will end up with Satan, the Antichrist, and the False Prophet in the Lake of Fire if they don't embrace it. And how will they hear without someone to tell them (Romans 10:14)? May you and I redouble our desire and effort to pull them "out of the fire."

And may our prayer be, with the apostle John, "Even so, come, Lord Jesus!" (Revelation 22:20).

1. Describe the setting of Luke 4:16–22. (When was it in Jesus' ministry; to whom was He speaking?)

   a. Compare the text of Isaiah 6:1–2 with Jesus' quotation of it in Luke 4:18–19. Find the key element from Isaiah that Jesus did not quote. (Hint: it's in Isaiah 61:2.)

   b. Why didn't Jesus quote that part of Isaiah's prophecy at this time?

   c. Separate the elements of Isaiah 61:1–2 into two categories: those pertaining to Christ's first coming and His second coming.

   Christ's First Coming   **Christ's Second Coming**

   d. How does Revelation 19:11–21 fulfill Isaiah 61:2b?

2. Read Isaiah 11:1–10.

   a. Divide the elements of this passage into those pertaining to the first and second comings of Christ (list them by verses).

   Christ's First Coming   **Christ's Second Coming**

   b. How do the prophets' visions parallel the way God sees time? That is, does God see past, present, and future separately or as one vision?

3. Why do the instructions of Isaiah 2:4 and Micah 4:3 not contradict the instructions of Joel 3:10? When were each intended to be fulfilled?

   a. How are Isaiah 2:4 and Micah 4:3 fulfilled in Revelation 20:1–6?

4. What promise is given in Revelation 22:7 concerning the prophecies of the book of Revelation?

   a. What motivation should that provide for studying and teaching these prophecies?

   b. How have the ten lessons in this series changed your own attitude about biblical prophecy and the future?

DID YOU KNOW?

George Frideric Handel's most well-known composition is *Messiah,* written in 1741, of which the most beloved section is the "Hallelujah Chorus." That chorus is based on three Scripture passages from Revelation that describe the Second Coming of Christ:

- 11:15 "The kingdoms of this world have become the kingdoms of our Lord and of His Christ, and He shall reign forever and ever!"
- 19:6 "Alleluia! For the Lord God Omnipotent reigns!"
- 19:16 "And He has on His robe and on His thigh a name written: KING OF KINGS AND LORD OF LORDS."

APPENDIX 1

Conventional Oil Reserves by Countries
June, 2007

Rank	Country	Proved reserves[1] (billion barrels) June, 2007	Percentage[2] world oil reserves
1	Saudi Arabia	264.3	21.9%
2	Iran	137.5	11.4%
3	Iraq	115.0	9.5%
4	Kuwait	101.5	8.4%
5	United Arab Emirates	97.8	8.1%
6	Venezuela	80.0	6.6%
6	Russia	79.5	6.6%
7	Libya	41.5	3.4%
8	Kazakhstan	39.8	3.3%
9	Nigeria	36.2	3%
10	United States	29.9	2.5%
11	Canada *	17.1	1.4%
12	China	16.3	1.3%
	Qatar	15.2	1.3%
	Total World Reserves	1,295,000,000,000[3]	

*When oil sands are included, Canada ranks #2 with 178.8 billion barrels of proved reserve. Currently oil sands are not traded on the US Securities and Exchange Commission, thus not included in the BP statistics.

[1] BP Statistical Review of World Energy. www.bp.com. June 2007. Accessed 3/4/08
[2] Ibid; BP Statistical Review of World Energy. www.bp.com. June 2007. Accessed 3/4/08
[3] Central Intelligence Agency; 2/28/08. www.cia.gov. Accessed 3/4/08

APPENDIX 2

Jewish Population Statistics
2007

Country	1970	2007	Projected 2020
World	12,633,000	13,155,000	13,558,000*
Israel	2,582,000	5,393,000	6,228,000*
United States	5,400,000	5,275,000	5,200,000
France	530,000	490,000	482,000
Canada	286,000	374,000	381,000*
United Kingdom	390,000	295,000	238,000
Russia	808,000	225,000	130,000
Argentina	282,000	184,000	162,000
Germany	30,000	120,000	108,000

* indicates anticipated Jewish population growth

Source: The Jewish People Policy Planning Institute: Annual Assessment, 2007. (Jerusalem, Israel, 2007)

Turning Point
Resources
by Dr. David Jeremiah

Escape the Coming Night:
The Bright Hope of Revelation

It is easy to dismiss the modern-day prophets who predict the end of the world. But then consider recent examples of world turmoil or modern decadence and silently wonder: Is this it? Is this the end? *Escape the Coming Night* is a penetrating look at the prophetic time machine that is in the book of Revelation, and a vivid reminder of how, in the face of coming darkness, we should live today.

Soft Cover Book REVBK *(Can - $14/UK - £13)*   **$13**

Study Guides
    Volume 1 REVSG1 *(Can - $11/UK - £10)*   **$10**
    Volume 2 REVSG2 *(Can - $11/UK - £10)*   **$10**
    Volume 3 REVSG3 *(Can - $11/UK - £10)*   **$10**
    Volume 4 REVSG4 *(Can - $11/UK - £10)*   **$10**
    4 Study Guide Package REVSGP *(Can - $35/UK - £32)*   **$32**

Compact Disc Albums
    Volume 1 (12 CDs) REVAL1CD *(Can - $86/UK - £55)*   **$78**
    Volume 2 (12 CDs) REVAL2CD *(Can - $86/UK - £55)*   **$78**
    Volume 3 (10 CDs) REVAL3CD *(Can - $72/UK - £46)*   **$65**
    Volume 4 (9 CDs) REVAL4CD *(Can - $65/UK - £41)*   **$59**

ORDER 1-800-947-1993

Turning Point
Resources
by Dr. David Jeremiah

Handwriting on the Wall
Secrets from the Prophecies of Daniel

Prophecy is more urgent and reliable than today's headlines. In this series, Dr. Jeremiah shows us how an understanding of prophecy can open the pathway to dynamic living. *The Handwriting on the Wall* delivers a story full of dramatic history, prophetic insights, and hope for today's Christians. Daniel, divinely inspired, accurately prophesied the rise and fall of empires and their rulers.

Soft Cover Book HOWBK *(Can - $14/UK - £13)*   **$13**

Study Guides
   Volume 1 HOWSG1 *(Can - $11/UK - £10)*   **$10**
   Volume 2 HOWSG2 *(Can - $11/UK - £10)*   **$10**
   Volume 3 HOWSG3 *(Can - $11/UK - £10)*   **$10**
   3 Study Guide Package HOWSGP *(Can - $26/UK - £24)*   **$24**

Compact Disc Albums
   Volume 1 (12 CDs) HOWAL1CD *(Can - $86/UK - £55)*   **$78**
   Volume 2 (10 CDs) HOWAL2CD *(Can - $72/UK - £46)*   **$65**
   Volume 3 (9 CDs) HOWAL3CD *(Can - $65/UK - £41)*   **$59**

Turning Point Resources

STUDY GUIDES

All Study Guides are regularly priced at $10

An audio album is also available for each of the following series.
(Sold separately. Individually priced.)

Acts: The Church in Action (4 Volumes)
Authentic Christian Life, The
  (1 Corinthians, 3 Volumes)
Basics of the Christian Faith
Blessings and Behavior of the Believer, The
  (Ephesians, 2 Volumes)
Captured by Grace
Celebrate His Love (Christmas)
Christians Have Stress Too
Christ's Death and Resurrection
Courage to Conquer
Escape the Coming Night
  (Revelation, 4 Volumes)
Facing the Giants in Your Life
Family Factor
Giving to God
God, I Need Some Answers
God in You (The Holy Spirit, 2 Volumes)
God Meant It for Good (Joseph, 2 Volumes)
Grace of Giving, The (Stewardship)
Handwriting on the Wall (Daniel, 3 Volumes)
Heroes of the Faith (Hebrews)
Home Improvement
Hope . . . An Anchor for Life
Hopeful Parenting
How to Be Happy According to Jesus
  (The Beatitudes)
How to Live According to Jesus
  (The Sermon on the Mount, 2 Volumes)
Invasion of Other Gods (New Age)
Investing for Eternity
Issues of the Home and Family
Journey with Jesus—The Life of Christ (3 Volumes)

Joy of Encouragement, The
Judges, The Book of (2 Volumes)
Knowing the God You Worship
Learning to Live by Faith (Abraham,
  2 Volumes)
Life Wide Open (Purposeful Living)
Living by Faith (Romans, 6 Volumes)
Living in the Light (1 John)
Looking for the Savior (Thessalonians,
  2 Volumes)
Miracles of Christ
My Heart's Desire (Worship)
Nation in Crisis, A (Joshua, 2 Volumes)
New Spirituality, The (New Age)
Overcoming Loneliness
People God Uses, The
People Who Met Jesus
Power of Love, The
Powerful Principles from Proverbs
Prayer—The Great Adventure
Ready! Set! Growth!
Runaway Prophet—Jonah, The
Searching for Heaven on Earth (Ecclesiastes)
Signs of Life (Authentic Christianity)
Signs of the Second Coming
Spiritual Warfare
Ten Steps to Spiritual Renewal
Tender Warrior, The (David, 2 Volumes)
Turning Toward Joy (Philippians)
Until Christ Returns (Prophecy)
What You Always Wanted to Know About Hea
When Wisdom Turns to Foolishness (Solome
When Your World Falls Apart (Psalms)

BOOKS

Angels: The Strange and Mysterious Truth $15
Captured by Grace $22
Discover Paradise $15
Escape the Coming Night (Revelation) $14
God in You (The Holy Spirit) $13
Grace Givers $15
Handwriting on the Wall, The (Daniel) $13
Hopeful Parenting $14
Joy of Encouragement, The $15
Life Changing Moments with God $17
Life Wide Open (Purposeful Living) $20
My Heart's Desire (Worship) $13
Overcoming Loneliness $13

Prayer—The Great Adventure $13
Prayer Matrix, The $10
Route 66 $10
Sanctuary (Daily Devotional) $14
Searching for Heaven on Earth (Ecclesiastes) $
Signs of Life $23
Slaying the Giants in Your Life $13
Things That Matter, The $10
Turning Points (Daily Devotional) $14
Turning Toward Integrity (James) $10
Turning Toward Joy (Philippians) $10
Until Christ Returns (Prophecy) $13
When Your World Falls Apart (Psalms) $13

POSTAGE AND HANDLING CHART	
For orders	Add
Up to $5.99	$1.50
$6.00-$19.99	$2.50
$20.00-$50.99	$3.50
$51.00-$99.99	$6.00
$100.00 & over	$9.00

For a complete catalog
of resources available from
Turning Point, visit
www.DavidJeremiah.org